ASEM
The Asia-Europe Meeting

Studies from the International Institute for Asian Studies
LEIDEN AND AMSTERDAM

Edited by
Paul van der Velde, General Editor

EDITORIAL BOARD
Prof. Erik Zürcher, Prof. Wang Gungwu
Prof. Om Prakash, Prof. Dru Gladney,
Prof. Amiya K. Bagchi, Prof. James C. Scott

PUBLISHED
HANI-ENGLISH, ENGLISH-HANI DICTIONARY
Paul W. Lewis and Bai Bibo

INDIA AND BEYOND
Edited by Dick van der Meij

DYNAMICS IN PACIFIC ASIA
Edited by Kurt W. Radtke, Joop A. Stam,
John Groenewegen, Leo M. van der Mey, Takuo Akiyama

NEW DEVELOPMENTS IN ASIAN STUDIES
Edited by Paul van der Velde and Alex McKay

A CONCISE HISTORY OF DUTCH MAURITIUS, 1598-1710
P.J. Moree

ASEM: A WINDOW OF OPPORTUNITY
Edited by Wim Stokhof and Paul van der Velde

FORTHCOMING
ABIA SOUTH AND SOUTHEAST ASIAN
ART AND ARCHAEOLOGY INDEX
Edited by Karel R. van Kooij

NEW ASPECTS OF ASIAN STUDIES
Edited by Paul van der Velde and Dick van der Meij

ASEM
The Asia-Europe Meeting

A WINDOW OF OPPORTUNITY

Edited by
Wim Stokhof and Paul van der Velde

KEGAN PAUL INTERNATIONAL
LONDON AND NEW YORK

in association with

INTERNATIONAL INSTITUTE FOR ASIAN STUDIES
LEIDEN AND AMSTERDAM

First published in 1999 by
Kegan Paul International
UK: P.O. Box 256, London WC1B 3SW, England
Tel: (0171) 580 5511 Fax: (0171) 436 0899
E-mail: books@keganpau.demon.co.uk
Internet: http://www.demon.co.uk/keganpaul/
USA: 562 West 113th Street, New York, NY, 10025, USA
Tel: (212) 666 1000 Fax: (212) 316 3100

Distributed by
John Wiley & Sons Ltd
Southern Cross Trading Estate
1 Oldlands Way, Bognor Regis
West Sussex, PO22 9SA, England
Tel: (01243) 779 777 Fax: (01243) 820 250

Columbia University Press
562 West 113th Street
New York, NY 10025, USA
Tel: (212) 666 1000 Fax: (212) 316 3100

© International Institute for Asian Studies 1999

Printed on Precision Fine acid-free paper
Printed in Great Britain
Jacket design by Jeremy Williams

All rights reserved. No part of this book may be reprinted or reproduced or utilized in any form or by any electronic, mechanical or other means, now known or hereafter invented, including photocopying and recording, or in any information storage or retrieval system, without permission in writing from the publishers.

ISBN 0-7103-0622-9

British Library Cataloguing in Publication Data
ASEM : a window of opportunity. - (Studies from the
International Institute for Asian Studies, Leiden & Amsterdam)
1. International relations and culture 2. International
relations 3. Europe - Foreign relations - Asia 4. Asia -
Foreign relations - Europe
I. Stokhof, Wim II. Velde, Paul van der
303.4'82
ISBN 0-7103-0622-9

Library of Congress Cataloging-in-Publication Data
A catalog record for this book is available
from the Library of Congress

FOREWORD

This publication is largely based on reworked versions of lectures held at the Wilton Park Conference on 'The Europe-Asia Relationship: How Could It Be Improved?', which took place from 1 to 5 September 1997. The conference was attended by some 50 specialists from Asia and Europe who freely exchanged their views on the emerging new Europe-Asia relationship. The conference was co-sponsored by British Aerospace and the International Institute for Asian Studies, Leiden and Amsterdam, the Netherlands.

This book contains eleven contributions, nine of which are slightly edited versions of lectures held during the conference. In order to obtain a more complete picture of the ASEM process we asked two other authors to contribute: András Hernádi, also one of the conference participants, was asked to write on the relationship between Asia and Eastern Europe; and César de Prado Yepes was asked to highlight a topic which, according to us, received insufficient attention during the conference, namely the influence of information technology on the ASEM process.

We have also added the Chairman's Statements of ASEM 1 and 2 and the Statement on the Financial and Economic Situation in Asia of ASEM 2, which was held in London from 2-4 April 1998. The readers will notice that in the articles the future tense is used when referring to ASEM 2. We decided not to change this because the articles were indeed written prior to that meeting.

We hope that this publication may serve as a small contribution towards furthering the promising new dialogue between Asia and Europe, not only in the ASEM framework but in other domains of society as well.

Wim Stokhof and Paul van der Velde

ACKNOWLEDGEMENTS

This publication would not have been possible without the enthusiastic cooperation and support of the staff of Wilton Park, Steyning (UK). Most likely influenced by the spirit of the ASEM process, the management decided to break with their longstanding tradition by actually consenting to publish lectures held at their conference centre, Wiston House. The surroundings were no doubt conducive to a free exhange of thoughts and ideas.

In particular we would like to thank the Chief Executive and Director of Wilton Park, Colin Jennings, and the Associate Director of Wilton Park, Robin Hart. The latter was the organizer of the conference on 'The Europe-Asia Relationship: How Could It Be Improved?', which took place from 1-5 September 1997 at Wiston House. The majority of the contributions to this book represent reworked versions of lectures held during that conference. We wish to thank all contributors to this publication for their insightful articles.

Furthermore, we would like to express our gratitude to Dick van der Meij MA, whose aid in copy-editing was indispensable, and to Gabrielle Landry for her English corrections on several parts of this publication.

The Editors

Contents

ASEM: A Window of Opportunity
Wim Stokhof and *Paul van der Velde*   1

THE POLITICIANS' VIEW OF ASEM

Setting the Agenda for ASEM 2:
From Bangkok to London via Singapore
Derek Fatchett   13

Strengthening Euro-Asian Relations:
ASEM as a Catalyst
Percy Westerlund   18

Involving Politicians in the Political Dialogue:
A Parliamentarian Perspective
Michael Hindley   27

IMPROVING MUTUAL CONTACT BETWEEN ASIA AND EUROPE

Bringing the Communities Together:
What More Can Be Done?
Wim Stokhof   35

Increasing Opportunities for Greater Contact:
Asia and Eastern Europe
András Hernádi   47

Connecting ASEM to the Global Information Society:
The Moving Scene
César de Prado Yepes   58

CHALLENGES AND PROBLEM AREAS

Getting Serious about Asia-Europe Security Cooperation
Dong-Ik Shin and *Gerry Segal*   73

Combating International Corruption:
In Search of an Effective Role for ASEM
Jong Bum Kim   84

Developing the Business Relationship between Asia and Europe:
Trends and Challenges
Tetsundo Iwakuni   95

THE FUTURE OF ASEM

Assessing China's Impact on Asia-EU Relations
Zhao Gancheng   109

The Future of the ASEM Process:
Who, How, Why, and What?
Jürgen Rüland   126

ANNEXES

1 ASEM 1: Chairman's Statement 1996   155

2 ASEM 2: Chairman's Statement 1998   162

3 ASEM 2: Statement on the Financial and Economic
  Situation in Asia   171

4 Contributors   176

5: Abbreviations   178

ASEM: A WINDOW OF OPPORTUNITY

Wim Stokhof and Paul van der Velde

The Asia-Europe Meeting (ASEM) is an unique interregional forum which consists of six members of the Association of Southeast Asian Nations (ASEAN), China, Japan, South Korea and the 15 members of the European Union (EU). ASEM officially came into being at the first summit, which was held in Bangkok in 1996. It was born out of a necessity, felt as much in Europe as in Asia, to improve the dialogue between both continents, which had been neglected since the end of decolonization. Although there had been contacts dating from the late 1970s at the level of foreign ministries between ASEAN and the EU, they were of a rhetorical nature and lacked substance. This has changed since the inauguration of ASEM. In general the process is considered by the parties involved as a way of fortifying the relations between Asia and Europe which is necessary to balance the triangular world (US, Asia and Europe) of the 21st century. Now that the process has been underway for two years we can begin to distinguish its main components which are, by far, more substantial than the talks between Europe and Asia before the inauguration of ASEM.

The main components of the process include political dialogue, security, business, education and culture. Since the first meeting of heads of state in Bangkok there has been a fair number of follow-up meetings on all the topics mentioned above. Political bodies generated some of these meetings but others spontaneously came into being. A number of the participating countries, realizing the importance of the process, have created ASEM sections within their respective ministries of foreign affairs in order to closely monitor the multi-faceted ASEM process. This is increasingly propelled by the many new opportunities for communication offered by the rapidly developing information technology.

Notwithstanding this positive start, ASEM remains a loosely organized process, which is an easy target for sceptics who often point to its non-focused nature. They are of the opinion that only the creation of a more formal body could secure the momentum of ASEM. Steps in the direction of formalization led to, for example, the creation of the Asia-Europe Foundation (ASEF) in Singapore in 1997. The ASEF aims at increasing the dialogue between Asia and Europe at all levels of society. Other initiatives such as the Asia-Europe Business Forum (AEBF) and the Senior Officials Meeting on Trade and Development (SOMTI) may well develop into more formalized bodies. Still the meetings of a more informal nature far outnumber the formalized ones and can be viewed as a token of the enthusiasm which the process has generated.

The articles in this book are a clear reflection of the more informal side of the ASEM process although not uniquely so. They are written by Asian and European politicians and academics involved in the process from its very beginning which all share the most important belief underlying the ASEM process, namely that it is based on partnership and equality. The contributions deal with a variety of topics such as security, economy, politics, education, culture, exchange of information and so forth. Of course these articles do not cover the whole spectrum of the ASEM process but they do give us an idea of what is not only an exciting experiment but which can also be construed as the beginning of a new era in the relationship between Asia and Europe.

The book is loosely grouped around four themes: The Politicians' View of ASEM; Improving Mutual Contact between Asia and Europe; Challenges and Problem Areas; and the Future of ASEM. The first three articles in this volume are concerned with the political dimension of the ASEM process as written by a Minister of State, a Director for Relations with Far Eastern Countries of the European Commission, and a Europarliamentarian. These contributions touch upon the various levels at which the political dialogue is taking place.

THE POLITICIANS' VIEW OF ASEM

Derek Fatchett, in his article 'Setting the Agenda for ASEM 2: From Bangkok to London via Singapore', reflects upon the Agenda of ASEM 2, which was held from 2-4 April 1998 in London. He clearly sees a special role in the ASEM process for the United Kingdom in bridging the gaps between Asia and Europe since it has been a long-time trading partner of Asia and since its economy enjoys much Asian investment. One of the aims of the British government is to further increase the comfort-level among the countries of ASEM, which was already high during the Bangkok meeting. This is now known as the 'Spirit of Bangkok'.

According to Fatchett, ASEM is unique because of the strong involvement of the business communities of Asia and Europe as exemplified in the AEBF. The involvement of business in the process will increase the prosperity of both regions and in a roundabout manner will also stimulate the political dialogue (also on sensitive issues such as human rights) which in Fatchett's eyes is at the heart of ASEM. Another cornerstone of the future success of ASEM is the broadening and deepening of educational exchanges between Asia and Europe. This is the most effective way to challenge existing prejudices and nurture new relationships. In this context Fatchett points to ASEF as a catalyst in stimulating cultural, educational, intellectual, and people-to-people contacts.

Percy Westerlund brings in the European Commission's perspective on how links between Europe and Asia can be intensified in his article, 'Strengthening of Euro-Asian Relations; ASEM as a Catalyst'. Although he is clearly optimistic about ASEM, he conceives of three possible trappings: the setting of unrealistic goals; proliferation of follow-up meetings; and holding summits too often. Of these three he considers the risk of proliferation as the most dangerous because he feels the process would then run the risk of losing its focus. In this context, Westerlund pleads for a structural approach along the lines of the comprehensive framework programmes applied by the EU in which priorities are clearly delineated. The establishment of the VISION group in 1997, which consists of resource persons from both continents, will lead to the formulation of such a programme. It will be presented during ASEM 3 in Seoul in the year 2000.

Although not necessarily in order of importance, Westerlund sees three priority areas: trade and investment; culture, education and personal exchange; and political dialogue. In the field of trade and investment there are now two main forums: the AEBF and SOMTI. Their task is to forge a Euro-Asian alliance in support of a more ambitious and global approach, and to advise the ASEM leaders and governments on how to improve economic ties. The SOMTI in turn is fed by two advisory groups, which will hand in reports on a Trade Facilitation Action Plan (TFAP) and an Investment Promotion Asia Plan (IPAP) during the meeting in London.

While the articles of Fatchett and Westerlund are written from a perspective of international politics, Michael Hindley, in his article 'Involving Politicians in the Political Dialogue: A Parliamentarian Perspective', deals with the question of how politicians should translate the ASEM process to the voters and subsequently how to generate enthusiasm for a fairly abstract phenomenon. Policies which seem to be rational and explicable at an interregional level do not necessarily always translate into positive scenarios at a local level. The lifting of measures restricting imports from Asia might well be conducive to the ASEM process but if in practice it boils down to, for example, the foreclosure of a plant with hundreds of workers in a parliamentarian's constituency, it will be very difficult for the politician involved to explain the grander political scheme and even more difficult for him to be re-elected.

Whereas such eventualities might diminish the popular support for ASEM, Hindley is also aware of the possibilities of democratizing the ASEM dialogue and commercial relationship by involving the population of Asian extraction in Europe in that dialogue. The European-Asians can play a key role into widening the ASEM dialogue, as can the politicians who represent them. Notwithstanding the fact that Hindley clearly understands the role of European-Asians in the process, he is not convinced that the advantages of a deeper understanding of each other's cultures are bound to improve the economic ties between Asia and Europe. However, many other people involved in the dialogue attach great value to the role culture can play in bridging the existing gaps between Asia and Europe. Wim Stokhof is one such person.

IMPROVING MUTUAL CONTACT BETWEEN ASIA AND EUROPE

In his contribution, 'Bringing the Communities Together: What More Can Be Done?' Stokhof focuses on the mediating role culture can play in increasing mutual understanding between Europe and Asia. Cultural rapprochement can only enhance the economic growth and deepen the political consensus. Knowledge of each other's cultures will augment our capacity to recognize prevailing stereotypes and to replace them by ideas and images which are deeply rooted in present-day realities. In order to be able to measure the impact of this process to some extent, Stokhof calls for a (permanent) survey executed across both regions, which could fine-tune the process of cultural rapprochement in the future.

Stokhof emphasizes the critical role education plays in the cultural sensitization. Therefore the exposure to each other's culture should begin at the secondary school level through the teaching of language and culture and the introduction of one-year fellowships for secondary school students to be carried out in Asia or Europe. At the university and institutional level, long-term joint research programmes on matters of interregional importance should be executed by mixed groups of researchers from Asia and Europe with disciplinary backgrounds in the Humanities, Social Sciences and in the technological field. The formation of strategical alliances between European and Asian research institutes could pave the way for such a development.

András Hernádi, in his article 'Increasing Opportunities for Greater Contact: Asia and Eastern Europe', looks at the possibilities of how to improve contacts between Asia and Eastern Europe. He draws a parallel between ASEM and Central Europe in the sense that ASEM is the missing link in a triangular power equation. In turn he considers Central Europe to be the missing link in ASEM itself. The Central European countries are by no means the only countries which are interested in becoming members of ASEM. More than twenty Asian and European countries also want to join in. Hernádi pleads for the inclusion of what he considers to be the core group of Central Eastern European countries: the Czech Republic, Poland, and Hungary.

Hernádi particularly looks at Hungarian relations with Asia. He predicts a shift of Asian investment from Western to Central Europe, which is more attractive in view of its low wage costs. Added to that, Hungary is a regional centre for tourism, banking and finance. Hernádi quotes three other assets of Hungary: its openness and multicultural set up; the Hungarian diaspora feeding back to Hungary; and the entrepreneurial and hard-working attitude of the Hungarians. He is strongly in favour of increasing the bilateral contacts with Asian countries by setting up centres in Asia, which combine diplomatic, commercial, educational and cultural efforts.

César de Prado Yepes, in his article 'Connecting ASEM to the Global Information Society (GIS)', treats a very important aspect of the future ASEM process. The emergence of the GIS creates a much wider range of opportunities for contact than ever before. Furthermore, these opportunities do not involve big expenditures. De Prado Yepes, like Westerlund, pleads for the adoption of EU-like framework programmes to achieve more focus. For example, in the sphere of communications there are endeavours such as in the Golden Bridge infrastructure project aiming at the informatization of China using advanced fibre-optic satellite technologies. De Prado Yepes is also strongly in favour of the creation of more Internet gateways in Europe and Asia because still now most Internet packet-switched traffic searching the fastest route to its destination finds its way through the US when flowing back and forth between Asia and Europe.

CHALLENGES AND PROBLEM AREAS

Dong Ik-Shin and Gerald Segal, in their contribution 'Getting Serious about Asia-Europe Security Cooperation', consider a more engaged approach within the ASEM towards security if it wishes to achieve a well-balanced global triangular relationship. Although Asia and Europe do not play an important role in each other's security context they do need to work more closely together in this arena. Segal and Dong Ik-Shin plead for a flexible understanding of the word 'security': economic and military dimensions can not be separated from it in an increasingly interdependent world. They distinguish between 'hard security' and 'soft security with and hard edge'.

After the withdrawal of the colonial powers from Asia there remains little of what could be labelled hard security apart from a few remnants of French and British presence in the area such as the Five Power Defence Arrangements (FPDA) in which the UK, Singapore, Malaysia, Australia and New Zealand cooperate. The sale of sophisticated weapon systems training and transfers of intelligence also fall in the 'hard' category. Since 1992 the European market share in arms (related) sales to Pacific-Asia hovers around twenty per cent. Dong Ik-Shin and Segal consider a sensible arms-transfer strategy of vital importance to security building in Asia. Defending a stable Pacific Asia that remains open and connected to the global economy is a vital interest of Europe which it should want to defend in order not to continue free-riding on the US.

In the field of 'soft' security they see three possible fields of cooperation in the ASEM context. The European countries have a wide experience in

Confidence Building Measures (CBMs) which they can easily share with their Asian partners. Also, European countries are very familiar with preventive diplomacy to help stop the emergence or escalation of conflicts, which can be valuable in the Asian context as well. The third field is peacekeeping operations in the context of the United Nations (UN). One-third of the budget and one-third of the personnel for such UN operations are from Europe. Asia's contribution to it is on the rise. Peacekeeping within the UN framework may enhance the ASEM process.

Another problem area (but at the same time an opportunity) for closer cooperation is international corruption. Jong Bum Kim, in his article 'Combating International Corruption: In Search of an Effective Role for ASEM', describes the recent international movement to combat corruption against the backdrop of the multilateral efforts to develop a framework for investment liberalization. In the process, he argues that ASEM can play a unique role by filtering the discussion on combating corruption before it reaches multilateral rule-making bodies such as the World Trade Organization (WTO). Kim proposes that ASEM should first take up the issue of combating international corruption before tackling domestic corruption issues. This has the advantage that the international community can avoid pointing fingers at corrupt behaviour in one particular country. Thus ASEM could first provide a balanced forum for raising consciousness of the adverse effects of corruption in international business and then could make concrete proposals to combat them.

Tetsundo Iwakuni, in his contribution 'Developing the Business Relationship between Asia and Europe: Trends and Challenges', makes a clear distinction in the relationship between overall trends, trade related trends and capital market trends. He then focuses in particular on the relationship between Europe and Japan, which he does not consider applicable to the rest of Asia. Iwakuni sees four major challenges affecting the future business relationship between Asia and Europe. These are related to the environment, the political culture, social ethics and education.

By far the biggest challenge lies in the field of education. Iwakuni points out that it is of crucial importance that the opportunities for educational exchange between Asia and Europe be drastically enlarged. Educational exchange is essential in ensuring mutual understanding in the areas of language, culture, economy and plain people-to-people contacts. Without this two-way flow it will be impossible to improve the relationship. He considers a challenge for non-English speaking countries in Europe to attract more Asian students. The number of Asians studying in Europe is a mere fraction of those studying in the US; while the number of European students studying in Asia is again a mere fraction of Asians studying in Europe. Not only the quantity but also the quality of the existing exchanges will have to be increased by including not only transfers of knowledge or technical skills but also the cultural background of the country the students are living in. In summary, raising the intercultural sensitivity by means of intercultural education is, in the eyes of Iwakuni, the paradigm on which the new Asia-Europe relationship should be founded.

THE FUTURE OF ASEM

Zhao Gancheng, in his article 'Assessing China's Impact on Asia-EU Relations', first examines China's domestic development in the past two decades and its recent open-door policy. Then he examines the important role China should play in the ASEM process. With its huge population and its fast-growing market, China does not only have a big influence on developments in Asia as a regional power but also increasingly as a global player. It is clear that China will benefit most from a stable Asia-Pacific as the EU does, but configurations at a regional level may interfere with those at a global level.

According to Zhao Gancheng China will work both towards improving its relations with other Asian countries and with the EU, which can be done effectively within the ASEM context. Therefore China will further open its markets and liberalize its domestic economy, which in turn will stimulate the economic relations between the EU, ASEAN, Japan and South Korea. Not only economic benefits will be reaped from this improved relationship: it will also create an environment in which security matters such as arms control and non-proliferation can be put on the agenda of ASEM. Furthermore, the new dialogue between Asia and Europe will help to balance the emerging triangular power structure of the 21st century.

In the last contribution to this book, 'The Future of the ASEM Process: Who, How, Why, and What', Jürgen Rüland looks at the future of the ASEM process in practical terms. As to 'who', it is no secret that a host of countries want to participate in the ASEM process for various reasons. Rüland singles out six categories of future participants: Australia and New Zealand; India and Pakistan; Russia; Eastern European countries; European Free Trade Association (EFTA) members; and Myanmar and Laos. As a yardstick for future inclusion in the process, he uses the argument that the candidates should not introduce new lines of conflicts which could endanger the process. In analysing the above-mentioned categories he does not anticipate danger in including Eastern European countries such as Poland, the Czech Republic and Hungary, Australia and New Zealand, and India and Pakistan because the *détente* between the latter two countries would be in the interest of all present ASEM members.

Rüland continues by pleading for a moratorium on membership until the year 2000. However, applicants should be given observer status and the secretary-generals of overlapping regional organizations should be unconditionally admitted to AEBF and ASEF. Furthermore, task forces should be formed which concentrate on the different aspects of the process. These in turn should feed back to the summits and the foreign ministers' meetings. In order to coordinate all activities, a modest secretariat should be set up (preferably in Bonn) and soon the allocation of the budgets will have to be sorted out.

Rüland puts forward a number of arguments both of a theoretical and practical nature as to why this process is functional and positive for all parties involved. As such the interregional approach in international relations promises to be the most fruitful in terms of efficiency. Multilateral bodies with too many players and too widely diverging interests have become unmanageable with rounds of negotiations, which can stretch out over decades. ASEM in particular can be a stimulus for the emerging triangular global power structure. Furthermore it can clarify intraregional positions on all kinds of topics and can increase the efficiency of international decision making.

Practical motives from a European point of view to actively stimulate the ASEM process are: making good for lost opportunities and recapturing the initiative in global affairs against the backdrop of its unification; using ASEM as a platform for discussion on issues which can not be solved at a supranational level; and shared security interests with Asia. From the Asian point of view, bolstering the ASEM process will increase its bargaining power with the EU which could become increasingly inwardlooking as a result of the unification of the 'fortressed' Europe. Asia could use ASEM to press for a more open economic system of the European Union.

As to what should be done in the future in the ASEM context, Rüland shares many of the ideas put forward by other contributors to this book. However, he clearly stresses that the involvement of civil society at all imaginable levels should be stepped up immediately because otherwise the ASEM process runs the risk of petering out. Needless to say, the media in Europe and Asia, which so far have paid remarkably little attention to this important process, should be more alert in picking up news that does not originate in the US but at our own doorstep in Eurasia. So the big question which remains to be answered is how popular the Asia-Europe Meeting really is.

ASEM FOR THE PEOPLE!

There can be no doubt about the fact that a new interregional dialogue between Asia and Europe, devoid of either colonial or new value rhetoric, is not only useful in the global triangular context but also *per se* as a means to boost the intraregional contacts of the Eurasian landmass and between two neighbouring cultures which were made to believe that they were of a completely different nature and texture. Such sayings as the 'East is East and West is West and never the twain shall meet' were engraved not only in the collective memory of the Europeans but also in that of the people of Asia. Going further back in time, a picture emerges of two cultures learning from each other and accepting each other. At the time, this took place on a very small scale. Looking towards the future we can not escape the conclusion that such a phase of cultural rapprochement is rapidly emerging, yet now on a more pervasive scale. Therefore the academic and cultural community should build on this new window of opportunity, which the ASEM process offers, by increasing communication at all levels.

Science and culture - the two most important cornerstones of the Eurasian civilization that brought into being a meaningful transfer, not only of people, but also of human matters such as ideas, technology, services, goods and food - must involve themselves across the board to integrate the challenge of the ASEM process. The process elevates the promise of a multicultural world in which twains stem from the same tree. It is not very likely that many people noticed the banner flying from Nelson's Column on Trafalgar Square during ASEM 2. The text written on it not only encapsulated the essence of the ASEM process but also its precondition for success: ASEM for the People!

THE POLITICIANS' VIEW OF ASEM

SETTING THE AGENDA FOR ASEM 2: FROM BANGKOK TO LONDON VIA SINGAPORE

DEREK FATCHETT

Never before has Europe's fascination with Asia been so powerful. I use the word 'fascination' because I think there is a genuine interest in Europe and in Asia in what these two very different parts of the world have achieved, and how they have achieved it. And while the media and academics speculate about the reasons for Asia's economic success, the long-term viability of that success can continue - though they will have to make real adjustments along the way.

Much of the debate about differences between Europe and Asia is clearly beneficial, opening up for us a greater understanding of Asian societies. But there are, I fear, certain shortcomings in the debate. I see two central questions.

The first is about the supposed differences between Europe and Asia. I become irritated by those who try to argue that there is one specific model of Asian values, based on hard work, the drive for success and the primacy of commercial relations. The notion that one continent falls within one model is stereotyping of the worst kind. A cursory glance at the different levels of economic development, at the varied political systems and the contrasting influences accredited to religions in individual countries, adequately draws attention to the challengingly varied characteristics of Asian countries.

We do not need reminding that we in Europe too start from different positions and have developed individual approaches to improving the lot of our peoples.

If deepening dialogue between Europe and Asia achieves anything, it should be to challenge outdated perceptions and stereotypes. Not least can it emphasize common 'themes'. We all want more economic development. Economic development means individuals becoming wealthier and wanting to gain more control over their lives. That can only be right. Diversity and innovation drive the world forward - and it is freedom of choice and control over their own lives which let people create diversity and innovation. That holds true in free market Asian economies as much as it does in Europe.

The second big question is, in my view, one which implies an entirely wrong and dangerous agenda. Too often, we seem to be asking what type of

Asia Europe wants. I am not surprised that so many in Asia find that question offensive and patronizing; the question, after all, does carry an echo of imperialist thinking.

Surely the real question, which the ASEM process and all our contacts should stimulate, is about the nature of an effective relationship between Europe and Asia. Defining what is effective in this context will not be easy. We do know, at least, that for a relationship to be effective, the element of partnership must be paramount: only through a sense of equality can debate be frank - and conclusions positive.

Partnership, however important it may be, relates only to process. We need to give some thought to substance. This is where the ASEM dialogue is so relevant. It offers the means to a broader relationship between the two regions, covering the key areas that matter to government, business and above all to our peoples. Furthermore, it offers that dialogue at all levels, from working contacts and cultural exchanges right up to the face-to-face meetings of leaders, as at ASEM 1 and soon at ASEM 2.

Maybe it is worth reminding ourselves that ASEM is a newcomer on the world stage - a potentially exciting newcomer if we have the vision to develop it successfully. The Singaporean ideas that gave rise to it bore their first fruit only in 1996 at ASEM 1 in Bangkok. That meeting proved to be a winner, not just in its organization but, more importantly, in its outcome. But it has set a standard and a challenge, especially for the UK as host of the first ASEM on European soil.

THE ROAD FROM BANGKOK

The achievements of ASEM so far speak for themselves. We have shown clearly the value of bringing together Asian and European leaders. The meeting defied those critics who said that it would simply be a source of friction. On the contrary, it was significant for the mutual respect and understanding which characterized the discussions.

At ASEM 1, the leaders of 25 nations and the European Commission demonstrated what has become known as the 'Bangkok Spirit': their mutual interest in working together, their determination to do so, and what could be achieved when they did.

Since then there has been an almost bewildering range of activities ranging from Ministerial Meetings and their supporting official meetings, to such imaginative ideas as young leaders' meetings, to more detailed work in, for example, customs cooperation and initiatives to increase trade and investment.

The process is still evolving. There is no shortage of new ideas. But perhaps there will be a need, as time goes by, for greater focus and better management.

However, the ASEM process already has one clear feature that distinguishes it from most other international processes: strong business involvement. So far this has taken the form of a Business Forum, a Business Conference, and consultation of business people on trade and investment initiatives. The next Business Forum will be in Bangkok in October 1997. We plan to hold a Business Event associated with ASEM 2 in London, which we hope will bring the concerns of business even more centrally into leaders' deliberations and into the very heart of the ASEM process.

Since ASEM 1, we also reached a major milestone in the Foreign Ministers' Meeting which took place in Singapore in February 1997. I would point to three particularly important results of that meeting. First is the progress that was made in political dialogue. If dialogue in ASEM is to achieve its full potential, it must be balanced and cover the full range of concerns we share. We were encouraged by the mature, mutually respectful and positive way in which political dialogue was tackled in Singapore.

For ASEM 2, we look forward to a high-quality political dialogue among the leaders, which will help to deepen their understanding of the issues that are important to one another and strengthen the Asia-Europe dialogue in a positive atmosphere. This should perhaps go without saying, after all, you may ask, what do our leaders discuss when they meet privately other than politics? But political dialogue has become something of a term of art in international affairs and can bring with it associations that not all find equally comfortable. Leaders at the Bangkok meeting made it clear that political dialogue was one of the key elements of ASEM. We see it as one of our tasks to help ensure that that dialogue takes place in the right way.

Secondly, the Singapore meeting discussed the complex question of membership. We have some way to go before partners will reach a consensus on the future shape and size of ASEM. The government of the UK has made no secret of its view that India, Pakistan, Australia and New Zealand would bring valuable new breadth and depth to ASEM. In Singapore, we agreed that no one had an automatic claim to membership. Discussions continue and, I hope, they will soon bear fruit. We hope that London will be able to take forward the debate on membership. It is not clear to me yet how far that debate will have developed by the time leaders assemble in London. It will necessarily be an issue of great importance, as it will help to define the future shape of ASEM.

Thirdly, Singapore also formally established the Asia-Europe Foundation (ASEF) to promote cultural and intellectual exchanges - the 'people to people' aspect of ASEM. We are determined that ASEM should not just be about government and business. If we are truly to build a bridge between the regions - and you will already realize that I believe strongly that we in the UK are well-placed to help that process come to fruition - the peoples of both regions need to know each other better, face-to-face, whatever the wonders of modern telecommunications may be.

The potential here is vast. We look forward to seeing an increasing stream of well-chosen cultural and intellectual projects backed by ASEF that contribute to the building of stronger Asia-Europe links.

THE ROAD TO LONDON

That is how we see ASEM's achievements. What of the future?

We in Britain are looking forward keenly to hosting ASEM 2. This will be a unique challenge for us: not simply to act as hosts for an important meeting, but also to demonstrate something in practical terms continuing long beyond the summit itself, that is, Britain's role in bridging the supposed gaps between Asia and Europe.

This may sound like a hollow boast. It is certainly a challenging task for us. But we have strong reasons to think that we can indeed succeed in strengthening the relationship between Asia and Europe. There is of course our history of involvement in the region, in particular as a long-standing trade partner.

But we can also offer many present-day strengths. We now enjoy a strong position in Europe, as many Asian countries have acknowledged by investing in Britain as a spearhead for their activities throughout the continent. Of course they are also attracted by our open economy: open to investors, traders and financial services. We are a tolerant, flexible nation. We have a political system which continues to evolve to meet changing circumstances. We are also a technologically advanced country with a track-record of innovation.

It should be no surprise, then, that we can look forward to building an even greater role in the future as a bridge between our two regions. The first major step will be the ASEM Leaders' Meeting in London in 1998. At that meeting, we hope ASEM will be able to make progress in all the main areas of work it has set for itself.

I have already referred to the earlier progress on political dialogue. It is the topic which is likely to raise the greatest interest. In the short-term, there will be a need for sensitive handling of the human rights agenda. At the ASEAN conference in July, there was debate about applying the universal principles of human rights. By all means let us discuss their implementation, but the key is that the fundamental principles set out in the Universal Declaration on Human Rights and in the UN Human Rights instruments should be applied everywhere. They are universal.

I mentioned right at the beginning the extent to which individuals whose economic needs are increasingly being satisfied will consequently wish to exert greater control over non-economic factors. This is a key long-term question in Asia as it has been, and is, in Europe.

At that stage, arguments which classify countries, especially those in Asia, as solely concerned with their economies will look even less well-conceived. I have no doubt that the future political dialogue in both parts of the world will include discussion of the best means to satisfy non-economic concerns. Future meetings of ASEM after London will no doubt play their part in this.

ASEM FUTURE AFTER LONDON

Finally, maybe I could also speculate a little about vision. I do not want to preempt the work which we expect to be launched with the Vision Group proposed by Korea. But I do want to encourage us all to look forward.

Let me first say that I recognize that vision, by definition, has a tendency to become so general that it relates to everyone - and no one in particular. But I hope that we can achieve something for the Asia-Europe relationship by seeking our vision through encouraging personal contact between peoples. That means contacts at every possible level, between every possible group: artists, academics, journalists, and captains of industry, to name a few. Children and students, too, should be involved: we attach great importance to educational exchanges. That is the most effective way we can challenge prejudices and nurture new relationships.

I am glad to say that the ASEM process is already developing this approach, through the inclusion of business people, through the informal face-to-face meetings of leaders which avoid over-bureaucratic methods and structures, and most notably through the involvement of the art world in a festival to take place alongside ASEM 2 with the support of the Asia-Europe Foundation. Through these contacts, ASEM will help begin to overcome the difficulties that geography imposes on cultural, intellectual, sporting, artistic and educational exchange.

Our vision must, then, be driven by one overriding consideration. We need to ensure that the prejudice, ignorance, and misunderstanding which can blight relations between peoples and between regions, have no part to play in the future contacts between Europe and Asia, at all levels. Historians talk about the 19th century belonging to the industrial revolution countries and the 20th century to the superpowers, especially the USA. Can we set ourselves a target that the 21st century stimulates new approaches of understanding and cooperation, with Asia and Europe in the lead?

STRENGTHENING EURO-ASIAN RELATIONS: ASEM AS A CATALYST

PERCY WESTERLUND

It is a sad fact that Europe has long neglected its relationship with the countries of the Asia-Pacific region, despite the fact that these countries have experienced a remarkable economic boom during the last few decades. Even relations with Japan, which were better-established than those we had with the rest of Asia, were until recently not as deep and comprehensive as one would expect from two major trading powers. There is really no good excuse for this, but there are several obvious explanations. The EU has been preoccupied with the challenges of deepening the integration process and of handling the revolutionary changes in Central and Eastern Europe. I think there may also be a problem of perception, in that the Europeans have only of late become aware of the spectacular growth in Asia. Trade and investment patterns clearly suggest that our American competitors have recognized and exploited the opportunities in Asia earlier than we did.

The European Commission has been aware of the need to upgrade relations with Asia. In June 1994, the Commission adopted a document on the EU strategy for relations with Asia. This paper had to be rather sweeping and general in substance, in view of the size and heterogeneity of Asia. But at least it gave a clear signal that we were beginning to appreciate the importance of Asia, not least as a market and as a powerhouse in the global economy. This document also sent a signal to our Asian partners that Europe was ready to establish a new relationship, based on equality and mutual respect.

The Asian response came only a few months later, in October 1994, during an official visit to France by the Prime Minister of Singapore, Mr Goh Chok Tong. Mr Goh suggested that a summit should be held with the leaders of the European Union and East Asia. The Asian-designated participants were the ASEAN countries, Japan, China and Korea. Singapore declared from the outset that the summit should focus primarily on economic cooperation. It was pretty clear that the Asian side saw APEC as a model for this new dialogue with Europe.

The EU quickly accepted the invitation and it was decided that the summit, called the Asia-Europe Meeting (ASEM), should take place in Bangkok in the spring of 1996. There was some initial disagreement as to the need for a political dialogue, but preparations were, generally speaking, without major problems. The actual summit was widely considered to be a major success. The personal chemistry amongst leaders was excellent and the media speculation about confrontation on political issues came to shame. Officials had prepared a Chairman's Statement containing some twenty follow-up actions to the summit. Leaders themselves spontaneously added half a dozen actions. It was decided that summits should be held every second year. The third summit will be held in Seoul in the year 2000.

WILL ASEM MAKE A DIFFERENCE?

The follow-up is already quite impressive, only eighteen months after the summit was held. But it could still be asked whether ASEM will truly make a difference. We have seen elsewhere that summits of this kind can trigger a sense of euphoria and lead to frantic activity, but more often than not this positive atmosphere has eventually been tainted by a sense of anti-climax. The most dangerous trap is probably the setting of unrealistic goals, which may seem so remote that no one feels the pressure to take any specific action soon. Another trap is proliferation of follow-up to cover almost all aspects of society, which often leads to wasteful duplication and premature institutionalization. A third trap is to hold summits too often. Summits can and should be catalysts for progress, but they will be counterproductive if there is not reasonable time to move the process forward in the meantime.

In preparing for ASEM, we have tried to avoid these traps. Summits are held only every second year and institutionalization has so far been avoided. The set objectives are realistic, but still useful. The problem is rather the rapidly growing number of follow-ups. There is quite frankly, a clear danger that follow-up activities will proliferate to the extent that we lose focus and sense of direction. We need to review priorities as well as the way ASEM initiatives are introduced, coordinated and monitored in order to ensure optimal results.

The services of the European Commission have recently put forward a working paper on ASEM follow-up for the consideration of member states, in which we pay particular attention to this problem. We suggest that ASEM adopt a so-called 'framework programme' at the next summit in London. This framework programme would identify the main priorities for the period between London and Seoul and also establish mechanisms to ensure that new proposals for follow-up be properly screened at lower levels before they are announced at ministerial meetings or summits by ministers or leaders. The idea of some kind of framework for the ASEM follow-up is mentioned in the

Bangkok statement and specific ideas on an economic framework have already been put forward by several Asian countries. Once we have agreed on a framework programme, which should be comprehensive, we will hopefully be able to better resist the temptations of proliferation and duplication. The framework programme will be complemented by a report by the so-called Vision Group of prominent Asians and Europeans, who will look at the medium and long-term objectives for ASEM. Their recommendations will be made in time for the third summit in Seoul.

What then should the key priorities be for the next few years? How can we best use the particular strengths of ASEM, its informality and high-level participation, to bring about the kind of follow-up that makes a difference? It should be stated at the outset that ASEM is not a negotiation forum and will consequently not conclude agreements. It can, however, function as a political catalyst and bring peer pressure to bear on participants. Such pressure could ideally lead to shifts in policy or even concrete action, which often would be taken unilaterally or in the relevant specialized multilateral forums. I will try to outline what I believe should be the key priorities in the next few years. I think these suggestions largely coincide with the views of the European Commission, but it goes without saying that I alone am responsible for the remarks I make here.

TRADE AND INVESTMENT

As I have already mentioned, trade and investment were very much on the minds of those who took the ASEM initiative. I do not need to elaborate on the great potential for trade and investment between Europe and the Asia-Pacific. Trade has already grown substantially, and so have investments. But European trade and investments in Asia are, relatively speaking, lagging behind. Asian investments in Europe are primarily of Japanese (and to some extent Korean) origin. Investments in these highly competitive markets are of great strategic importance, both with regard to future trade flows and for the ability of companies to stay abreast with technological and commercial developments.

The economic dynamism of Asia is particularly striking. The predictions are mind-boggling. Several reputable institutions, including the World Bank, have predicted that China will catch up economically with Japan within the next few decades. The implications of such a development, if it were to take place, are underscored by the fact that the Japanese economy today is about ten times as large as that of China. The World Bank has predicted that about half of the world's economic growth will take place in the Asia-Pacific region by the year 2000. I would predict, however, that we would also begin to see rather high and sustained economic growth in Europe over the next few years. Painful structural changes in Western Europe will pay dividends, as will the opening of markets in Central and Eastern Europe. The realization of the EMU will further stimulate investment and growth in Europe.

From all this follows that it is one of the most important tasks of ASEM to raise the awareness, among Asian and European businessmen, of this great potential. Beyond this, ASEM should also try to promote specific measures, which could facilitate and stimulate trade and investment. Let me first comment on the awareness raising. I think that ASEM is well equipped for this task, thanks to its informal networking at very high levels. There is a special 'club-like' atmosphere in ASEM, which is essential for successful international cooperation. Closer ties at the political level will help strengthen Euro-Asian ties at all levels of society.

We have already seen how the commitment at the highest political level has helped strengthen ties among business communities. A good example of this was the inaugural meeting of the Asia-Europe Business Forum (AEBF), which was held in Paris in October of last year at the invitation of President Chirac. Thanks to the strong commitment of the French government, the AEBF meeting in Paris became a great success. Top executives from both regions initiated a very useful and practical dialogue, which will continue when the next AEBF session takes place in Bangkok in November 1997. The EU would like to see AEBF become the core forum for private sector participation in ASEM. Its role should be to strengthen bonds between business communities and advise ASEM leaders and their own governments on what needs to be done to develop our economic ties to their full potential.

ASEM can also help spur trade and investment between the two regions through liberalization and specific facilitation measures. With regard to liberalization, I think there is broad agreement among partners that it should primarily be achieved through the WTO. The role of ASEM should chiefly be to help build consensus for renewed multilateral action, perhaps even a new global round in the next few years. Admittedly, regional and sectorial liberalization can also benefit the trading system as long as WTO rules are observed. But experience shows that global rounds of trade negotiations produce the best results. The most difficult trade issues, such as agriculture and textiles, can only be effectively addressed in a broad negotiation package and with all-important trading nations involved. Having said this, I would of course not exclude that ASEM or other regional forums could make useful contributions to liberalization. But the main objective should be to forge a Euro-Asian alliance in support of a more ambitious and global approach.

Work is already well under way when it comes to promotion and facilitation of trade and investment between Asia and Europe. Only months after the first summit in Bangkok, there was an initial Senior Officials Meeting on Trade and Investment (SOMTI) in Brussels. It was then decided that four partners, Korea, the Philippines, the Presidency of the Council and the Commission, would elaborate a proposal for a Trade Facilitation Action Plan (TFAP). We are still working on this plan with our Asian partners, but there seems to be broad agreement between the two sides on about half a dozen priority areas for trade facilitation (facilitation of customs procedures, harmonization of standards and norms, public procurement, facilitation of sanitary rules, IPR and putting a 'virtual marketplace' on the Internet). For each priority area we will try to identify several specific objectives, which should be achievable between the next two summits. These 'achievables' should represent concrete and useful improvements for the business community, but they should also be realistic goals. SOMTI will be in charge of monitoring the implementation of TFAP. An expert group may be created to review progress and then report to SOMTI.

Officials recently agreed, in principle, on the content of an Investment Promotion Action Plan (IPAP), which had been asked for by leaders at the summit after a proposal by Thailand. IPAP identifies certain measures to promote investments in general terms between Europe and Asia. It also sets out a plan to look at how the regulatory framework affects foreign investment. This latter point has been a priority for the EU, since we do believe that a sound, stable and predictable regulatory framework is essential for the confidence of investors. Some Asian partners were initially sceptical, perhaps because they thought they had no problems attracting investments anyway. We were able to agree on a way forward, however, once it was clarified that ASEM would and could not negotiate binding rules. Again, one of the advantages of this dialogue will be its potential for preparing the ground for later WTO negotiations. It will also be useful for governments to learn more about the specific investment impediments encountered by companies on either continent. We hope that the Asia-Europe Business Forum will be able to help provide officials with such specific information. I think we will find this dialogue very beneficial, regardless of how far investment issues can be taken in the WTO.

An expert group will be created also for the implementation of IPAP. It will report to SOMTI. Both TFAP and IPAP will be reported to the London summit, and the implementation of these two action plans should be top priorities for follow-up in the trade and investment area until the summit in Seoul.

CULTURE, EDUCATION AND PERSONAL EXCHANGES

The so-called 'cultural gap' between Asia and Europe is widely seen as a major obstacle to a closer relationship between the two continents. Leaders very much highlighted the need to strengthen ties between Europeans and Asians, and particularly among students, to help bridge this gap. I think this is perhaps the most important aspect of the ASEM follow-up. If we can enhance contacts and create key networks among the future leaders of our societies, then we have also made a major investment in our future political relations and business ties.

A lot has already happened in this area. Even before the first ASEM summit, the first Asia-Europe Cultural Forum was organized in Venice in January 1995. This conference, which also had non-ASEM participants, was interesting and useful in that it helped illustrate the complex nature of the cultural gap. It also helped dispel the myth of Asia and Europe as cultural monoliths. This interesting dialogue, with ranking participants from government, business and academia, will be continued in Manila in December of this year.

The Japanese government took the initiative to hold the Asia-Europe Young Leaders Conference, which first took place in Japan in March of this year. This initiative ties in with the idea of establishing a network of future leaders at an early stage. Another meeting of this kind will be held in Austria next spring.

On the occasion of the meeting of ASEM Foreign Ministers in Singapore in February of this year, the Asia-Europe Foundation (ASEF) was launched with financial pledges amounting to USD 15 million from ASEM partners. Substantial additional support is expected from the private sector. ASEF has been set up to support Euro-Asian cultural events and personal exchanges of the kind indicated above. ASEF should have a very important role as an engine for ASEM efforts to bridge the cultural gap. An initial meeting to discuss ways of strengthening the academic networks between Asia and Europe was held in Naples early 1997. Another meeting was held in Kuala Lumpur later that year. As I indicated above, the strengthening of student and academic exchanges is perhaps more important than anything else for the future of Euro-Asian relations. There is no reason why we could not eventually develop student exchanges with Asia to the same level as our exchange with America. ASEM should not undertake any major initiative of its own in this area, but rather stimulate participants to do more and to streamline existing activities.

The Commission is preparing for an important initiative of its own in this area. The idea is to offer a kind of student scholarship, which hopefully, over time, could help to significantly strengthen economic ties between Europe and Asia. There are already several programmes for this purpose, such as the Executive Training Programme with Japan and the Junior Managers Programme with the ASEAN countries. They are all excellent and highly regarded programmes, but they require a long and demanding commitment by participants. These programmes are also quite costly and hence also limited in participation. The new project, called the Asian-Europe Business Internship Programmes, would offer young business school students internships in European affiliates in Asia during the summer holidays. Similar internships should be offered to Asian students in Asian companies in Europe. The internships would be complimented by a programme on the political, cultural and economic life of the host country. This internship programme would offer but a foretaste of Asia or Europe, but it could have great spin-off effects on career choices if the students are young and receptive. By making the programme short and inexpensive, we would hope to develop the kind of volume exchange, which is needed to make a difference. A feasibility study is already under way for pilot projects in China and Japan, which we would hope to be able to launch in 1999.

Political Dialogue

As I have already indicated, some Asian partners were initially less than enthusiastic about a political dialogue in ASEM, perhaps because they feared that certain sensitive issues might come to the fore. The EU, on the other hand, has insisted that this new relationship between Europe and Asia would be incomplete without a political dialogue. Leaders eventually agreed in Bangkok on the need for a political dialogue and even gave some guidelines for it.

Progress has so far been rather limited, even though a very open and constructive discussion on the format for the political dialogue took place at the Foreign Ministers Meeting in Singapore earlier this year. Asians cautioned that this dialogue had to develop gradually and they stressed the need to develop the right 'comfort level' before addressing more sensitive issues. There is now, I think, a better understanding of each other's perceptions. Europeans realize that Asians would like them to listen more and lecture less on political matters. Asians, on the other hand, have hopefully begun to accept that a genuine new relationship between Europe and Asia, based on equality and mutual respect, must also allow for exchange of views on difficult or sensitive matters. I am personally optimistic. I think that the positive and constructive atmosphere of ASEM, known as the 'Spirit of Bangkok', will gradually produce the comfort level needed for this kind of dialogue. I would therefore hope that the next summit could lead forward to an interesting and substantive dialogue. In fact, such a substantial dialogue could even get started already at the next Senior Officials Meeting, which will take place in Luxembourg in October 1997.

The difficulties in developing a political dialogue do, to some extent, reflect the cultural gap I touched upon earlier. Conversely, it is clear that a broad-based and serious political dialogue is essential to the greater task of bridging this gap. The political dialogue should therefore be stimulated not only among ministers or senior officials. One method of broadening the political dialogue, which is explicitly mentioned in the Bangkok Chairman's Statement, is to promote dialogue and networking among think tanks in Europe and Asia. A lot of activity has already developed spontaneously in this field. The Commission is itself planning to contribute to this academic dialogue through a seminar on economic security issues early 1998.

It should also be underlined that we already have a good and constructive political dialogue with most ASEM partners within the frameworks of our bilateral relationships. In addition, the EU participates actively in the political dialogue of the ASEAN-PMC and the ASEAN Regional Forum (ARF). Still, we feel that we would fail to achieve the kind of comprehensive relationship indicated as a goal in the Bangkok statement if we do not have a political dimension to ASEM.

I might add that there is an interesting political dimension to ASEM, which goes beyond the question of political dialogue. ASEM is different from APEC, not only because the latter has no political dialogue. The eighteen 'member economies' of APEC participate individually and without any regional coordination. It is true that ASEM is not about a relationship between two 'blocs', but there is a certain regional coordination before important meetings. There are even two so-called 'coordinators' for each side (Commission and Presidency of the Council for EU, currently Japan and Thailand for Asia), who are in charge of internal coordination. This is standard procedure for the EU. ASEAN, too, has a certain tradition of internal discussions and even coordination of positions on both political and trade issues, but this is the first time such an Asian dialogue also includes Japan, China and Korea. Through this internal Asian dialogue, ASEM may not only bring Asia and Europe closer together, but could also help improve relationships among Asian countries.

CONCLUSION

I would like to stress two things. The first is that ASEM should not and will not replace or overshadow our various bilateral relationships with Asian partners. On the contrary, I would hope that ASEM would help further vitalize bilateral relationships. This follows from the informal nature of ASEM. It is an excellent forum for sending political signals and for the concerting of efforts, but the end results of ASEM will often depend upon implementation at the bilateral level.

Second, I would like to stress that we are acutely aware that Europe and Asia are larger entities than the sum total of ASEM. Leaders stated at the Bangkok meeting that ASEM should be an open and evolving process. There are already around 20 applicants from both Asia and Europe. The general attitude towards enlargement is positive, but there is not yet full agreement on procedures and the pace for it. There is concern about too rapid enlargement, particularly at a stage when ASEM is still being consolidated. ASEM already has 26 participants and could easily double in size if enlargement is not undertaken in a deliberate and measured way.

Let me finish by saying that I feel confident that ASEM will become a very important vehicle for the promotion of Euro-Asian relations, granted we manage to stay focused on the key priorities and avoid the temptation of proliferation in the follow-up. The growing importance of relations between Europe and Asia is mainly due to irrefutable economic realities. Even without ASEM, they would increasingly make themselves felt. The important role of ASEM is to promote and facilitate this trend. In a world economy dominated by the three poles of Europe, North America and East Asia, we cannot afford to let one of the legs in this triangle become much weaker than the others.

Involving Politicians in the Political Dialogue:
A Parliamentarian Perspective

Michael Hindley

The document from the International Institute for Asian Studies circulated for this conference starts with a typically sound, pragmatic and cautiously optimistic article by Singapore's Premier, Mr Goh. Mr Goh stresses the potential for commercial growth between Asia and Europe, emphasizing - rightly, in my opinion - the view that in a tri-polar trading world, that is, Asia, North America and Europe, it is the Asia-Europe side of the triangle which is the weakest. Mr Goh then advocates the need for cultural awareness positing the unproven thesis that cultural awareness increases trade possibilities. Alas, I find no convincing evidence of this in history. Cultural awareness is desirable. It is certainly necessary, for it can offset the malign forces of feelings of racial superiority and prejudice inherited from the colonial history and which still blight Europe's relations with the wider world. However, there seems to be no evidence at hand that such abiding cultural deficits actually upset trade and investment. I know it suits academics, threatened with potential redundancy in the harsh world of market economics visiting the university campuses, to argue for a new role for themselves teaching trade related cultural awareness, but the evidence does not seem to be there to justify this change in their intellectual emphasis. I still think there is a strong case for the traditional, liberal teaching of different value systems, but not to enhance trade.

The traders of the world have always got on well enough without an intellectual excuse; making money alone keeps them well fired-up. For example, the vast numbers of businessmen disgorging into burgeoning Chinese coastal cities are no more culturally aware than their colonial predecessors. That, however, does not seem to inhibit their success. Their crudity may be resented but it does not dissuade the Chinese from doing profitable business with them. I have heard many tales of crude Western behaviour, but no tales of such behaviour leading to the cancellation of contracts - although I would sincerely like to be contradicted on this point.

Mr Goh also makes point of broadening the dialogue between Asia and

Europe, using particularly the vehicle of ASEM for this purpose.

The Premier mentions ministers in this dialogue, mentioning also the curious fact that ASEM began at the highest political level. Mr Goh advocated drawing into the dialogue academics, media people and cultural leaders. I do not dissent for a moment, but I read on in vain for a mention of elected politicians. What role are they to play in this dialogue? It is on that which I shall try to concentrate.

Britain's former Foreign Secretary, Douglas Hurd, a man of vast and admired diplomatic experience and skill, made a very interesting point in his broadcast memoirs on the BBC, when he said modern politicians needed more time. Superficially there is more contact, not just by the tremendous growth and facility of telecommunications, but statespersons are now constantly jetting off for high-level conferences, for diplomatic rounds of new initiatives. But is there really any more understanding? There is certainly more consensus around the things which seem possible and realizable in the post-Cold War world. Douglas Hurd contrasted this kind of activity to the older form of diplomacy where international conferences took months and the Foreign Secretaries rented villas and took some time to socialize. Everyone acknowledges that the value of the first ASEM summit in Bangkok was the possibility for small groups to meet, disperse, reassemble with different partners, move on and regroup. This is not merely a plea for all of us politicians to be part of a permanent travelling conference round, but democracy does need time, and time is money. Democracy has to be paid for and the effort would be rewarded.

It is important for another reason too, and that is that it is always the domestic politicians who eventually have to explain to the voters and the citizens what has been decided by the great and the good at the higher levels. The grander ideals and strategies for a new world order need endorsement and it is the elected politicians who are the necessary intermediaries in that process of popular underpinning of international relations. This can be neglected at peril. It is frequently forgotten nowadays that Woodrow Wilson's remarkable *tour-de-force* at Versailles failed to get the endorsement of his own Congress and the resultant absence of the USA from the League of Nations crippled that worthy body from the very beginning.

All too often I find in my own experience that politicians are often left explaining something they are not too sure about themselves to an even more sceptical public. There is a pressing danger in this new world economic order of ours, that what may well be necessary for the good governance of the world, has well outstripped that which public opinion is ready to digest.

I often hear voices from outside politics that politicians should resist popular pressure; this is the world turned upside down, for surely politicians were invented to articulate popular pressure. Politicians are natural communicators and their undoubted skills and valuable connections must be recruited to popularize, not vulgarize, the complex issues which increasingly face us in an ever more closely integrated world economy.

Let me say a general word about Asia-Europe. At the moment there remains considerable ambiguity centred essentially on the question as to whether, from a European perspective, Asia is a threat or an opportunity - a competitor or a cooperator. Often tension can be creative; between the USA and the European Union (EU) there is clearly a feeling of mutual interdependence but also of rivalry. Indeed commercial rivalry is a vital stimulus to invention, innovation, and competition. But there is not in Europe, apart from certain sections of French society, the sense that the USA is a threat. When we look towards Asia, however, there is a strong feeling that Asia's recent and future expansion is at our expense. The rhetoric of mutual benefit is there, but the day-to-day reality is very different. The French have been particularly successful in Europeanizing their own anxiety about their ability to compete and this has frequently turned into demands to protect 'European industries' (e.g. French subsidized car makers). I think it is vitally important that European politicians sympathize and articulate these contradictory pressures without becoming prisoner to them.

Let me say a word now as to how the elected politicians in the European Parliament (EP) contribute to the trade-making policy. The European Union has a degree of pooling of sovereignty unique in history, especially in the field of trade. It is the EU Commission which represents the member states in multilateral trade discussions like the GATT, and in drawing up bilateral trade agreements with individual countries or regional groupings like ASEAN. When the Council of Ministers issues a negotiating mandate to the Commission, the European Parliament must appraise that mandate. Further, the Commission must keep Parliament informed during the negotiations and finally, when an agreement has been drawn up, that trade agreement needs the approval of the European Parliament and the ratification of the Council of Ministers. The Council can, and has, enacted agreements before or without waiting for Parliament's approval. However, given the growing need for what we call 'transparency' to overcome the 'democratic deficit', it will inevitably become harder and harder for the Commission and the Council to act without the seal of popular approval by the Parliament. It is the Parliament, which receives the growing amount of mail of disapproval and anger about the relative human and social rights situations in the third countries, with which the EU draws up its trade agreements.

Such a process causes intense annoyance for many Asian countries, which frequently complain about hostile resolutions from the European Parliament. I do not want to make too much of an earlier point, but what are politicians for if not to pass on the genuine complaints and worries of their constituents? If my post bag contains many letters of concern after an exposé of an alleged abuse of human rights somewhere in Asia, it is my duty to pass those on; it is not my role to pass on to my constituents the excuses and explanations of the government concerned. That is the job of that country's diplomatic corps. Certainly - and here parliamentarians are vulnerable to criticism - I do have a duty to check the veracity of those stories. Recently the EP has aroused the wrath of the Chinese government for making such criticisms, and complaints have been made about the EP's timing. Again I must make the simple point that democratic assemblies cannot be asked to control their 'timing' in order to spare the alleged embarrassment of diplomats.

Certainly Western democracy is and always will be somewhat random in its attention to subjects. The perceived insult is often not meant; the hidden meaning may indeed not even be there. In my own dealings with Chinese politicians, I am often reminded of the old story of how you can never convince a plotter that there is not a plot. The anecdote of Metternich at the Congress of Vienna is highly apposite: When told that the Pope had died, the arch plotter mused, 'Why do you think he has done that?'

There is no question in my mind that in improving the East-West dialogue, the term 'Europe' is a convenient fiction. The EU is still more disparate than it pretends, but as everything is relative, the EU is a good deal more cohesive than any other grouping. Using a collective persona of 'Europe' certainly helps us progress beyond the still sensitive atmosphere accruing from our colonial past. Virtually every European state has something to be ashamed of in its colonial past in Asia, and to be frank, none is immune to criticisms of abiding neo-colonialism. However, a collective persona as 'Europe' does allow the dialogue to transcend a blighted past. This has been useful in the case of China where 'Europe' provides a neat counterbalance to Chinese apprehensions of being overly dependent on either the USA or Japan. The collective 'Europe' has a useful and attractive neutral aura.

Unfortunately, particularly in the case of ASEAN, there was a dislocation in the late 1980s, for just when East Asia and Southeast Asia began to take off spectacularly and began looking for a partner, Europe itself became introverted, understandably, as the EU concentrated on the surprising but welcome reunification of our continent. All the EU's strategic planning was predicated on the seeming permanence of the Cold War, which meant that Eastern Europe was, to all intents and purposes, virtually closed for Western interests. With that welcome change, which, as I always remind audiences, was not achieved by high diplomacy or summitry, but by an exercise in people's power, Western Europe had a new and urgent task which diverted us from the wider world. Now that the former Soviet bloc, particularly Central Europe, is relatively stable and indeed applying for membership to the EU, perhaps the EU can pay due attention to developments in Asia once again.

Finally, let me turn to how we can in the best sense democratize the dialogue and commercial relationship between Asia and Europe. We now have, particularly in my own country but also elsewhere in Western Europe, a considerable population of Asian extraction. That population, now into its third generation from emigration, has developed considerable political, intellectual and economic acumen.

There are already tremendous informal links, but to my mind we have not really tapped into this potential. We must press for a popularization of that widening ASEM dialogue which so far has been successful, to draw in larger numbers of those people in the EU who actually understand from their inheritance how to deal with Asia. It is politicians who represent and are in touch with that potential and it is politicians who must now be trusted with a wider and creative role in developing better understanding between Asia and Europe.

IMPROVING MUTUAL CONTACT BETWEEN ASIA AND EUROPE

BRINGING THE COMMUNITIES TOGETHER: WHAT MORE CAN BE DONE?

WIM STOKHOF

I am pleased to have the opportunity to present some aspects of the current state of cultural contact between Europe and Asia and I will endeavour to give an assessment of what currently is going on, both officially and between people and institutions involved in studying, teaching, or practising the essential aspects of culture in all its variety in both regions. Having done so, I will reflect briefly on the role of culture as a pivot in achieving the objective of strengthening relationships between Europe and Asia, and I will (try to) make some suggestions for (new) approaches and initiatives for the future. At this conference, I sometimes get the feeling that talking about Asia often boils down to talking about the Asian countries participating in ASEM. I believe this is most unfortunate. Central Asia and the Indian subcontinent are clusters of states which cannot be ignored.

I define 'culture' here, in the broad sense, as the whole set of thinking and action patterns, which are distinctive features of a group. 'Cultural rapprochement' is the process and the results of mutual acquaintance of the respective cultures. Sometimes I use culture in the more generally accepted, limited sense, as a set of features primarily pertaining to the artistic process (cultural practice) and its products to distinguish it from other phenomena such as education, information, and diplomacy.

As you will have noted from the programme of this meeting, these reflections on the process of cultural rapprochement between Europe and Asia are being presented and discussed alongside similar assessments of the economic and political links between the two regions. In view of the forthcoming ASEM 2 in London 1998, I am happy to note that the question, 'What can be done to enhance a greater understanding and awareness between the people and decision-makers of both regions?', receives the attention it deserves. Mind you, in the context of the process of European integration, we are now regretting not having paid proper attention to the cultural dimension at an earlier stage, choosing instead to concentrate most of our time and energy on economic and technological integration without doing much about persisting stereotyped images and perceptions the people and decision makers in neighbouring countries in Europe might have of each other. I believe that towards the end of his career, the founding father of the EU, Schumann, admitted having regrets in this respect. Of course cultural rapprochement between Europe and Asia is not the same as cultural understanding within Europe *per se*. However, the analogy, in the sense that in the Europe-Asia relationship everybody tries to jump on the economic bandwagon, is obvious.

WHAT IS GOING ON IN ASIA-EUROPE CULTURAL EXCHANGE?

Since the announcement of the EU Asia Strategy of 1994, initiatives aimed at enhancing cultural relationships between Europe and Asia have grown considerably in scope and momentum; up to the point that the heads of state and government from both regions expressed their commitment to cultural rapprochement at the first Asia Europe Meeting in Bangkok in 1996.[1]

In the wake of the ASEM in Bangkok, Singapore and France undertook preparations for an Asia Europe Foundation (ASEF). A high profile promotional tour to Europe by Singapore's Prime Minister in late 1996 was followed by the ASEF founding declaration in February 1997, with funds voluntarily pledged from most of the twenty-five ASEM countries, worth over 15-20 million USD. A Board of Governors and national advisory committees have been formed, an Executive Director, Prof. Thommy Koh, has been appointed, and the ASEF Secretariat is in the process of being established. Acting as a clearinghouse and information centre, the ASEF will facilitate interactive linkages between academics, artists, cultural groups, scientists, students, media personnel and think-tanks. It will also support initiatives undertaken by founding members and organize a number of flagship activities in respective fields of interest, which can be broadly labelled 'culture'. It is my impression, however, that the ASEF will be mainly restricting itself to short-term flashy exercises generating a high degree of visibility. Apart from these initiatives at the intergovernmental level, the EC is coming forward with new programmes aimed at bringing the societies of Europe and Asia together by supporting private, local, or regional links at all levels of civil society, particularly in the cultural, educational, and information sectors.[2]

Some specific cultural and educational cooperation programmes at present in the portfolio of the East and South/Southeast Asia Directorates of DG I are:

1. a cross-cultural and economic cooperation programme, EU-India, involving the media sector, the educational sector, and entrepreneurial networking;
2. a EU-ASEAN Junior Executive Managers exchange programme;

3. European Studies Programmes in Thailand, the Philippines, (more countries in preparation);
4. a higher education programme in China;
5. an EC-China Business Management Institute in Shanghai;
6. an ASEAN-EC Management Centre in Brunei Darussalam;
7. production of EC-wide directories of existing linkages;
8. making an inventory of modern Asian Studies in Europe;
9. organization of EC-Asia forums, colloquiums, and seminars.

Subsidiarity to existing bilateral programmes between nations of both regions and complementarity to civil society initiatives are the basic principles underlying these regional programmes. They are endorsed by programme flexibility and adaptability indispensable in view of the great variety in cultural and educational institutions in both regions.

Turning to links between European and Asian institutions, I could refer you to the directories and inventories mentioned above, pertaining to Asian Studies, research partnerships, cultural centres, foundations, etc.[3]

In this context, mention should be made of the work carried out by the International Institute for Asian Studies (IIAS) in setting up a European Database of Asian scholars on behalf of the Asia Committee of the European Science Foundation. It will be published in 1997 and contains more than 5,000 Asia specialists and approximately 1,000 institutes and organizations in the field of Asian Studies. The IIAS also produces a newsletter on Asia with global distribution, manages fellowship programmes and conference agendas and is making preparations for a European Asia Resource Centre in cooperation with the Nordic Institute of Asian Studies (NIAS) in Copenhagen. It goes without saying that the IIAS is undertaking these activities as much as possible in line with growing institutional links between Europe and Asia in the economic and political sphere. It is very interesting to note that all these signs of an increasing focus on Asia have surfaced in the past five years.

All well and good you might say, but it may be of no less importance to be more responsive to the overwhelmingly increasing intensity generated in relationships between the people living in both regions. Mutual understanding may be only partly addressed by providing the right information to the right decision makers and practitioners. Undeniably, it also depends on the appreciation of cultural expressions and practices between the two regions where different values and norms are applied. The real substance of cross-regional cultural contacts is in the mobility of people in both directions; their mutual exposure to media, film, performing arts, exhibitions, architecture, design and fashion, and tourism; their awareness of the different life styles, food habits, and working practices; their appreciation of each other's youth cultures; and, like it or not, their disputes over expatriate job competition, migration, religious confrontation and racism (apart from the conventional trade and security disputes).

In short, exposure to each other's cultures is a precondition for increased mutual understanding.

So to briefly reiterate: the official cultural programmes, the institutional initiatives, and the common contacts between the two regions are converging. A multitude of actions at each level is building up into a wave composed of tokens of mutual interest and stated commitments to follow these up: Will we be riding this wave or be caught in the dump?

WHAT ARE THE FUNCTIONS OF CULTURE IN THE ASEM PROCESS?

The foregoing leaves no doubt that cultural rapprochement is now recognized as an important dimension in the pattern of Europe-Asia relations at all levels of interest and covering all areas of attention, both in terms of cultural knowledge and of cultural practice. The EC, particularly the DG I (External Economic Relations, Asia Directorate), describes this relationship as the first pillar in the strategy to construct economic cooperation with Asia. A similar perspective is included in the founding declaration of the ASEF where you can find cultural exchange described as the fourth pillar of the Asia Europe House. Percy Westerlund even called it the most important aspect of the ASEM process.

Let me quote from an overview of university relationships presented by the EC DG I Asia Directorate recently presented in Helsinki: 'In the framework of the economic cooperation between Europe and Asia, the general objective is to improve the economic, social and cultural context by creating a climate of confidence'.[4] Involving a broad range of cultural and educational institutions in cross-regional relationships is expected to create the most propitious atmosphere for the nurturing of a long-term partnership in which economic and political ties will flourish. The notion of a climate of confidence alone indicates a long-term perspective. But even in the short and medium-term, this is expected to enhance mutual understanding and underpin existing economic and political relationships both interregionally and bilaterally.

I agree with these views, but I must emphasize that this should not be understood as some sort of linear sequence in which sharing values leads to enhanced economic relations and then political cooperation. Actually, a debate concerning the role or functions of culture in support of other types of relationships will only fragment our understanding of the overall pattern of Europe-Asia relations. Causal thinking carries its own risks when the perceived functional effect does not eventuate, remains invisible, or backfires. We should also not be tempted to idealize the cultural dimension; just because of the recent wave of negative opinions triggered by Huntington's 'Clash of Civilizations' thesis.

However, we do note that the attention paid to cultural issues in Europe-Asia relations at the level of official policy, institutional activity, and popular involvement, is increasingly converging at this particular juncture in time. We do not want to make the same mistake I referred to above, made at the beginning of the foundation of the European Union. Instead of neglecting the cultural dimension in our relationships, there is ample opportunity for deriving mutual benefit from paying more attention to this area.

ARE THESE HIGH EXPECTATIONS OF THE ROLE OF CULTURE JUSTIFIED?

Cultural rapprochement as such does not automatically generate economic activity. But since there is already an enormous political interest, cultural rapprochement can only enhance the economic growth and deepen the political consensus.

The potential for mutual respect and equality is inherent in the universal appreciation of culture, regardless of differences in economic and political power that might affect the relationship. The undertaking of cultural relationships generates new tissue into which new commercial and political relationships between the regions can be interwoven; cultural contacts may help to open up new channels and areas of interest, provide for understanding and awareness between the partners (perhaps even temper things which go amiss), and prepare future generations for a role in these relationships.

Furthermore, now the influence of interregional cultural relationships at all appropriate levels can be expected to be higher than at any other time in history, owing to the enormous expansion of electronic communications and both the virtual and physical mobility of people who are exposed more and more to each other's life styles, food practices, design and technology, to a point at which one could almost speak of hybridization. In other words, what is the level of the Europeanization of Asia and what is level of Asianization of Europe? Needless to say, the tremendous possibilities of communication created by the Internet do not automatically improve mutual understanding. On the contrary it could duplicate the already existing stereotypes.

Culture is playing a mediating role by increasing our alertness not only to the facts and figures we need to know about our partners, but also in terms of enhancing our understanding of contemporary issues and events in both regions, thus enabling us to come to grips with stereotypes and distorted images, particularly those negatively affecting the overall relationship between Europe and Asia. To mention a few outstanding issues.

REGIONALIZATION AND GLOBALIZATION

Culture is part of the present stage of 'getting to know each other' as part of the ASEM process as defined by the Singapore Prime Minister, Mr Goh Chok Tong, in his Brussels lecture of October 1996. Both regions are being tied into processes of adjusting regional governance structures and institutions and increasing their contacts with other regional entities and global structures (EU, ASEAN, SAARC, APEC, NAFTA, and UN). This requires, like it or not, tackling cultural issues head-on, cooperating in regional forums and establishing partnerships with other regions in support of these processes.

The increasing openness within Asia may enhance the willingness and capacity there to deal with other relationships, particularly with Europe. By participating in international networks and cross-regional partnerships, Europeans and Asians are able to compare their own ways of dealing with each other and themselves. Two examples: the Vietnamese dealing with the French may find solace in learning from Koreans or Indonesians how they cope with the French; the Dutch may profit from looking at the way English and the Germans deal with Indonesians.

STEREOTYPES AND MUTUAL IMAGES

Of course the exposure to telematic communications and the mobility of travellers in both regions both have the same implications. The difference is that both of these developments directly influence people's consciousness and perception of mutual images in the global setting. I am not a political scientist adhering to the American school; in fact I am a linguist and just a director of the IIAS. I have no pretensions whatsoever of bashing Huntington's dire predictions of cultural clashes or of formulating a containment strategy along the 'fault lines' as he seems to recommend.

I simply have an interest in cultural diversity in all its manifestations. If only for expanding means of communication and the concomitant necessity to address questions of cultural identity and to do away with stereotypes, paying due attention to cultural issues is more than justified.

To tell you the truth, I believe that we do not even have a clear picture of our mutual images, apart from a high score for the 'Asian miracle' myth in the European (and American) media and an equally high score for the 'European decline' myth in Asian media. The only substantial survey of Europe's image in Asia that I am aware of, is a 1994 BBC survey of Asian perceptions of Europe, which was commissioned by the EC in preparation of the launching of its New Asia Strategy.[5]

Over and above this, through regular polls run by the *Far Eastern*

Economic Review and *Asiaweek*, we are informed of the perceptions of Asian executives and decision makers on issues pertaining to Asian affairs. These polls are useful instruments for the purpose of improving European images of Asia, provided these publications are more widely read in Europe. For instance, a stereotyped image of Asian collectivism and subordination to authority faltered when, in a recent FEER poll, the majority of Asian executives declared that they place a very high value on working for personal progress and individual freedom.

I strongly believe that we must make a mutual effort to get rid of the prevailing stereotypes in which Asia is seen as the ultimate sweatshop, the USA as the quintessential powerhouse and Europe as the public museum.[6]

Not only do we lack a clear understanding of the most cherished perceptions of our friends, we are also lacking an overview of what we are doing together at present and how the public appreciates this.

THE ASIAN MIRACLE?

The growing attention paid to cultural issues is of particular relevance to the ongoing debate on the sustainability of the 'Asian miracle', which was started some years ago by Krugman in *Foreign Affairs*. As you all know, Krugman presented his thesis of Asia's economic eclipse/saturation as a consequence of intensified resource exploitation without growth in productivity. Today, Asia's slackening (but still high) economic growth rates, its mounting (but still manageable) current account deficits and financial risks, its infrastructural bottlenecks, and above all its dependency on export revenues from ecologically damaging natural resource exploitation and socially damaging low-wage industries, seem to vindicate Krugman's thesis.

Yet, other analysts have argued the opposite, proclaiming the beginning of an 'Asian Golden Age'. The role of Asian values has been highlighted in this context, which is yet another debate I will not go into on this occasion, except perhaps, to argue again that I appreciate this as recognition of the importance of culture as an entity in its own right. Leaving aside whether Asia is overcoming the present setbacks or whether it will reach its Golden Age, these matters cannot be resolved without addressing certain tasks which have strong cultural implications.

To wit:

a) improving the quality of human resources (technological, managerial, legal, financial);
b) adjusting key institutions and regulatory frameworks.

Following the points made above, you may agree with me that the strengthening of Europe-Asia relations in the realm of culture involves more than just trying to smoothen the process of forging economic and political ties and/or to balance the weight of the relationships between Asia and other parts of the world, particularly the USA. Parallel mutual efforts in view of the points just mentioned above (a and b) are crucial to the flourishing of cooperation.

Which New Approaches in Cultural Rapprochement?

Regardless of whether cultural relationships between Europe and Asia are concerned with official programmes or activities of institutions such as universities, research centres and think-tanks, media agencies, corporate business, civic and cultural institutions, I could propose five common criteria to be observed in our future endeavours:
a) emphasis on equality in partnership, cooperation and mutual encounters, by undertaking cultural initiatives within the scope of official framework agreements;
b) subsidiarity and proportionality of official initiatives balancing bilateral or civic relationships between Europe and Asia, by focusing on cross-regional and pan-regional themes and issues;
c) medium-to-long-term perspectives aimed at creating a climate of confidence by involving younger generations as future partners in areas of mutual interest;
d) multi-level approaches linking official programmes to institutional and individual initiatives and encounters, including those established through long-distance communication, tourism, student and staff mobility, and other exposure to cultural products;
e) and multi-sector approaches involving the study and practices of culture.

Framework Agreements

Turning to framework agreements, it is clear that these are indispensable instruments to guarantee a comprehensive initiative, long-term commitment and, above all, equal decision-making authority at all stages of the formulation, design, implementation, and evaluation of cultural exchange relationships. From this point of view, as I mentioned before, cultural exchange is particularly opportune because of the mutual 'demand' factor in the context of regionalization and globalization. It is a promising area because of the inherent equality of cultural partnerships, both in terms of substance and, to an extent, in terms of institutional capacity and potential availability of funds.

SUBSIDIARITY AND PROPORTIONALITY

When it comes to the notions of subsidiarity and proportionality, an explanation may not be necessary here at Wilton Park, except perhaps a few words to underline that these notions apply with particular force to situations of cultural diversity in the twenty-five nations involved in the ASEM process. All ASEF or EU-ASEAN initiatives in this area will be measured by their value-added impact in comparison to bilateral cultural agreements and programmes and private institutional linkages. This may depend largely on whether official programmes focus on the regional dimension, both in terms of substance and in terms of method. In this respect it is important to distinguish between what is interregional value-added and what is intraregional value-added. The intraregional processes provide the experience that can be applied to the interregional process and vice versa.

MEDIUM-TO-LONG-TERM PERSPECTIVE

The medium-to-long-term perspective may be seen in the context of the notion of creating a climate of confidence between Europe and Asia, which can best be done through the younger generations, and in the context of cultural relationships between Asia and other parts of the world, particularly the USA. Here again, Europe seems to be at a disadvantage in comparison to American cultural and educational products, but this may also be turned into an advantage, as there is a growing feeling of 'USaturation' among the emerging middle classes and the elite in the region. The strategic consideration is to define what is value-added in the EU-Asia cultural exchange in view of America's hegemony in exporting mass consumption patterns, educational and media products. This is not an argument for launching a cultural competition or extolling Euro-chauvinism, but simply one for restoring a balanced pattern of EU/Asia/USA triangular relations, leaving ample scope for hybridization on the basis of positive experiences with the other regional partners.

It is worthwhile to note that in contrast to the US, Europe shows a wide diversity in academic traditions and scientific approaches. This pluralism guarantees a nuance in the way of looking at the world. Add to this the gigantic collections of manuscripts, libraries, archives, and the many museums and a well-organized academic infrastructure, it may well be a reason for our Asian friends to reconsider their main orientation towards the US. Europe is a treasure-trove for Asian Studies.

As for the European context, we consider it of utmost importance to introduce, at an early stage of the secondary school level, awareness courses pertaining to Asia: the introduction of Asian languages such as Chinese, Hindi,

Japanese and Malay to sensitize Europeans in their youth to things Asian. This suggestion is all the more important in view of the paradoxical situation that, while interest in Asia at the European level is on the rise; the programmes in the field of Asian Studies (languages, Social Sciences) are on the decline.

MULTI-LEVEL AND MULTI-SECTOR APPROACHES

The increasing convergence of official programmes, institutional activities, and individual encounters between Europe and Asia may be a blessing for those who have long advocated an increase in the attention paid to this trend, but inevitably it requires some concentration of means and coordination of activities in both regions. Accordingly, the recently created Asia Committee of the ESF aims to achieve a cogent concentration of force amongst universities, national umbrella organizations, think-tanks, cultural institutions, business schools, and development studies institutes with an interest in Asian affairs.

A greater embedment in society at large can be achieved by combining theory and practice of culture in meaningful manifestations, which allow material, and immaterial aspects of culture to converge. So far, and now I am talking as a scholar, international forums of Asianists have been extremely inward looking. This is the moment to introduce fluidity as a key concept in the organization of such gatherings. For example, during the first International Convention (ICAS) of Asia Scholars in 1998 which is being organized by the IIAS, a combined film and music performance, an Asian poets session, and a South Asia documentary film festival are part of the programme. Everyone can attend these events. Thus, different sectors of culture and society will have the opportunity to interact.

Taking into account these principles, a strategic alliance between European and Asian institutes specifically is suggested, working along three lines of operation:

a) to establish the necessary critical mass required to manage large Euro-Asian research programmes of the kind needed to deal with today's global issues (themes mentioned include environment, health, employment and changing labour relations, linguistic diversity, religion, democracy and political institutions, security issues, trade, finance and investment). It is our experience in the Netherlands that long-term joint research projects are a very useful tool to create mutual insight and trust between researchers. It may help to build up a multi-faceted Asia-Europe research culture, which could have tremendous impact on students generated by this research;

b) to pool the existing knowledge into European information resource centres on Asia and vice versa (offering surveys of public opinion, directories and institutional profiles, newsletters, documentation, and Internet services);

c) to coordinate new initiatives aimed at specific user groups and the general public (carrying out policy-related analyses; participating in EU-level conventions and forums, briefings and lectures to diplomats, corporate business managers and media; disclosure of collections; organization of exhibitions; servicing twinning programmes and alumni associations; and producing awareness programmes aimed at secondary educational institutions); and to introduce Asian languages at the secondary level of education so as to make people aware of Asia at an early stage of their lives.

These are the steps I suggest, but first an action to measure what we really think of each other (or how we are led to think by studies and media reports), is called for after four years of frantic activity in both regions involving getting to know each other better. The expressions of commitment by thousands of selected key individuals participating in interregional exchanges and forums may, or may not, have had an impact. A professionally executed survey across both regions is called for because this is undoubtedly the only way to measure the impact of our activities and to fine-tune our future actions to achieve optimal results.

Secondly, action is needed to analyse the accumulated result of the surveys and databases now available. The output could help determine which thematic areas are in need of further development, or the contrary, and which might be the most appropriate role for national or international umbrella organizations in view of the principle that official programmes should endorse institutional and private encounters, instead of being a substitute for these.

In any case, national (and regional) umbrella organizations should have the capacity to manage (hopefully relevant or well-appreciated) interdisciplinary research programmes and multi-sectoral cultural activities for the benefit of decision makers and the general public in both regions. But they should also play an active role in the process of Europe-Asia rapprochement and people-to-people relations between both regions by establishing broad-based membership and catering to genuine constituencies of organizations and individuals with an interest in Asia. In short:

1. cultural sensitization in Asia and Europe at the secondary school level through language and culture teaching;
2. clustering of Asia Studies know-how and expertise at a Euro-Asian level;
3. highly-developed and expanded exchange programmes for all levels of society;
4. long-term joint research programmes;
5. the establishment of strategic alliances between the main institutes in the field of Asian Studies in Europe and Asia;
6. a survey of European conceptions of Asia and of Asian conceptions of Europe as further cultural rapprochement.

Notes

1. To recall, the Cultural Forum of Venice in January 1996 was a milestone as it was conducive to creating the atmosphere of mutual commitment at the ASEM in Bangkok. Other EU-Asia forums, on Science and Technology and University Cooperation, have been organized in Engelberg, Munich, Naples, Helsinki, and Manila.
2. The recent EU Communication 'Creating a New Dynamics in EC-ASEAN Relationships' specifically links the strengthening of cultural and educational relationships to the ASEM process.
3. Specifically *'Directory of Inter-academic partnerships European Union Asia'* by Europrospective (1996); *'Educative, Linguistic and Cultural Policy of Cooperation with the ASEAN'* by European College for Cultural Cooperation and, as an example of a national product: *'East and Southeast Asia related Research at Finnish Universities and Institutes of Higher Education'* by National Network University for East and Southeast Asia Studies (1997).
4. EC-ASEAN Round Table on Education and Training, Helsinki May 25-28.
5. 1994 BBC survey.
6. Paraphrased from the *Far Eastern Economic Review*'s question 'Will as the waggish prediction has it, Asia become the World's factory, America the World's supermarket and Europe the World's museum', *FEER*, 10 July 1997.

INCREASING OPPORTUNITIES FOR GREATER CONTACT: ASIA AND EASTERN EUROPE

ANDRÁS HERNÁDI

The invitation to Wilton Park, followed by the one to contribute a chapter to a book on ASEM, has really been an honour not only for me, but for my country as well. As you definitely know, neither Hungary, nor any other country from among the group of former socialist countries has been accepted as a member of the ASEM dialogue yet, not even in an observer's capacity. I do know, of course, that no such category exists in the former documents of ASEM, but in a world of change and dynamism perhaps the concept itself could be amended. This is not only because it is, in my view, of vital interest for Central European countries to become a part of the ASEM process as soon as possible. I would also dare to argue that if ASEM is to supply the 'missing link', as it is often referred to, to tri-lateralism in our world, Central Europe could just as well supply the missing link to ASEM itself.

It is easy to note when looking at its present 'membership' that ASEM, on the European side, does not include any countries outside the European Union, as opposed to the non-ASEAN members in Asia. However, as ASEAN by its recent extensions towards Indochina has opted for including some newer and in fact poorer neighbours, the EU has also expressed its readiness to receive into the European House some Central European countries in the years to come. Even if the argument seems to stand that additional members to the ASEM dialogue, if for none other than practical reasons, might slow down the dialogue, no one knows, however, whether the process itself might not gain momentum by the inclusion of newcomers who might also serve as mediators between the two sides.

In any case, I did notice that I seem to have entered, right at the outset, one of the most sensitive issues of the dialogue (i.e. the issue of membership). Having gone through this book, it must have become clear to any reader that it seems to be the Asian side's turn for newer members now, as they are still fewer around the table. One should not forget about the size of the countries, and especially their populations, who are already in. Furthermore, in the spirit of open regionalism, Asian member countries might be flexible enough to accept some of those still out. It might at least be worth giving it a try.

EASTERN EUROPE?- DEFINITIONS DO MATTER

There are far too many definitions of what should be considered Eastern Europe. Instead of adding another one to those in circulation, I would rather suggest a very simple and logical concept, which would try to combine geography with political and economic aspects. Along these lines, and with utmost simplicity and much less scientific quality, I would say the core-group of Central Eastern European countries are those which were first invited to enter both NATO and the EU (i.e. here and hereafter strictly in alphabetical order: the Czech Republic, Hungary and Poland). Interestingly enough, the same countries have established the strongest ties with the EU and countries in the Far East. The second group in Central Eastern Europe comprises Romania, Slovakia and Slovenia. These are the 'almost-made-it' ones but which are still kept on the waiting list by NATO and/or the EU. Drawing the circle wider would involve Estonia, Latvia and Lithuania from Northern Eastern Europe, and Albania, Bulgaria and the rest of former Yugoslavia from Southern Eastern Europe - by no means on an equal footing with each other, yet in quite similar geopolitical situations. The last threesome, Belarus, Moldova and Ukraine, does not seem to have much chance of joining either NATO or the EU in the foreseeable future, and as such these might be defined as Eastern European countries. Finally, there is Russia, the only country which geographically does belong to both Europe and Asia, and whose membership in ASEM has, therefore, already been considered, but very clearly objected to as well.

In my view, it is only the Central Eastern European countries, and mainly their above-mentioned core-group, which could first be accepted around the table of ASEM. Their closeness both in time and space to the European side of ASEM, on the one hand, and their historical experience with the type of socialism still in place in China and Vietnam, on the other, as well as certain traits so characteristic of their population, but also often associated with 'Asian values', might all serve to help the two sides find compromises in the course of the ongoing dialogue. Technicalities like more translation work could easily be dispensed with, as the respective politicians could and experts of all the three countries have by now become accustomed to carrying out international negotiations in English. What is equally important is that, while devotedly working on their full membership in the EU, they all pay special attention to the Far Eastern region in their foreign economic policies.

In what follows, I shall argue for the significance of and the opportunities for greater contact between Central Eastern Europe and the Far East on the basis of my own background. As a Hungarian economist who has been conducting research on the Asia-Pacific region for more than twenty-five years, I should be in a qualified position to do so. I hope to live up to my own expectations and to those of the readers.

CENTRAL EASTERN EUROPE: A BRIDGE TOO FAR OR TO THE FAR EAST?

In order to illustrate that it is not only in my interpretation that Central Eastern Europe plays an important role in the context of the Europe-Asia relationship, let me call attention to a point of most surprising relevance, put forward by Professor Akira Kudo, University of Tokyo, in his study on the changes in the economic relations between Japan and Europe.[1] The collapse of the Japanese political regime of 1995 '... may be seen as part of the chain reaction to the European upheaval.' On the other hand, '... the Japanese economy has grown too large to be neglected in explaining the present socio-economic upheaval in Europe. On the contrary, Japan's economic power has been one of the important factors responsible for triggering the upheaval. In fact, European efforts to unify the European Community market by the end of 1992 might be said to have been undertaken primarily as a European response to the economic challenge posed by Japan. One might also say that the collapse of the socialist systems of the former Soviet Union and Eastern Europe was prompted, to a large extent, by the weakening of their economies under the overwhelming impact of the rapidly growing economies of East and Southeast Asia with their close links with Japan's economy and private firms.'

Thus, it is not necessarily correct to believe that the Central Eastern European countries, especially the ones mentioned in the core-group, should be handled as latecomers to the ASEM process which should not be allowed to disturb the ongoing 'performance', but told to wait to take their seats in one of the intervals only. They have always played their role in the history of Europe and had, in fact, made quite notable contributions to it. Before being misunderstood, let me point out that my argument is not aimed at acquiring sympathy for these three countries, rather to persuade both sides of the ASEM dialogue of the advantages of drawing them into the process. At a certain moment though, perhaps after their reaching full membership in the EU, it will be absolutely anachronistic to keep them away, and a gradual inclusion, for example, an observer's status or a consultative one with no veto rights (like the one offered to them by NATO as of January 1, 1998), would be beneficial for all sides.

Looking at the latest trends of foreign direct investments by, and perhaps more importantly the future plans of, Asian companies to invest in Europe, one can clearly see an increased readiness to choose one of the core-group countries (i.e. the Czech Republic, Hungary or Poland). TDK, Sony, Toyota and Daewoo are just a few flagships soon to be followed by others. Another emerging trend foreseen, with little chance of being mistaken, is the step by step withdrawal of Far Eastern companies from Western Europe into these Central Eastern European countries where wage costs, even corrected for productivity and capital intensity, are much more attractive. New trade and investment bridgeheads will be established in the years to come.

A recent authoritative analysis by UNCTAD[2] has listed the reasons why Central and Eastern Europe offer unique opportunities for investment locations for Asian firms as follows:

* to overcome current and expected import protection from part of the European Union;
* to maintain their cost advantage *vis-à-vis* domestic European Union producers;
* to make use of the strong local demand for manufactured goods and of the cost edge stemming from local production; and
* to utilize the stabilized economic and political conditions that have created a more favourable environment for foreign direct investment.

Judging by trade and investment figures of the past, there is an immense opportunity for entering the markets of the above threesome, especially when one takes into consideration their capacity to grow and, together with this, the growing demand for infrastructural development and durable consumer goods. The sudden change that has taken place in the structure of foreign trade of these countries after their historical changes in the late 1980s (i.e. a brisk move from the East to the West)[3], might soon need some fine-tuned (re)adjustment. When that process is to unfold, the most dynamically developing Far Eastern countries, hungry for consumer and capital markets, will give another push, even the ones which had to face a severe setback due to their recent financial troubles.

HUNGARY: A CASE-STUDY OF FACTS AND CHANCES

Hungary's trade with the Far Eastern countries, not much different from that of the other two Central Eastern European core-group countries, might be a case in point. As shown by Table One, Hungary badly needs a breakthrough in its Far Eastern foreign trade, because:

* even its originally low share in exports (3.4 per cent) went further down (to 1.6 per cent);
* the total value of exports has also decreased drastically (from USD 328 million to USD 202 million);
* the 'healthier' adjustment of its imports has led to a trade deficit surpassing USD 700 million (in fact, 30 per cent of the total deficit of Hungary in 1995).
* trade with, and especially exports to, former 'friendly' or even 'brotherly' countries like the PRC and Vietnam has also gone down.

Table One
Hungary's Foreign Trade with Far Eastern Economies
(in millions of USD)

EXPORTS   IMPORTS

	1989	1995	1989	1995
Japan	111	77	141	339
People's Republic of China	117	22	92	126
Hong Kong	13	20	11	47
Taiwan		8	.	126
Republic of Korea	18	9	36	146
Singapore	6	9	16	35
The Philippines		2	.	4
Indonesia	16	24	27	21
Malaysia	6	13	13	34
Thailand	23	9	9	27
Vietnam	18	9	14	11
Trade with '11'	328	202	359	916
Hungary's total trade	9.674	12.860	8.883	15.483
'11'/Total (%)	3,4	1,6	4,0	5,9

Source: *IMF Direction of Trade Statistics Yearbook*, 1996
Note: Data for the year 1996, only available from quarterly and 'mirror' statistics of IMF, show no difference in trends.

Hungary's share in the trade of the same 11 Far Eastern economies was almost negligible (expressible only in tenths, hundredths or thousandths of a per cent) and, due to the dynamically developing turnover in Asian countries, it has also decreased, making the use of a table for illustration unnecessary here. The share of FDIs by the two biggest investors from the region, Japan and the Republic of Korea, was not more than 5 per cent of the total at the end of the period under review.[4] Thus, one can point out that the two-way relationship is rather a matter of future opportunities than one of past successes, but the chances are there indeed.

Notwithstanding the recent financial crisis in some of the Southeast Asian countries, even they and the other economies of the region have a higher-than-average medium and long-term growth potential, sufficiently based on their realistic development plans and an ever-increasing consumer demand. At the same time, economies with the largest foreign exchange reserves in the world (Japan, the PRC, Taiwan and Singapore) also belong to this group of Asian countries, putting them into an excellent position to look for investment opportunities abroad.

More specifically, the huge Japanese economy, even with its smaller growth potential (2-3 per cent), is still strong enough to have backward and forward linkages to the other Far Eastern economies, although a newer momentum will now be coming from the rest of the region towards Japan. Therefore, a sense of partnership stemming from the strengthening of interdependence will develop. China's growth prospects are still good, even if some slowing down (to the range of 6-8 per cent) in the medium-term seems very likely to occur due to bottlenecks in the economy and structural changes coming to the fore. Hong Kong's new position will keep it on the strong side (never mind the loss in the prices of PRC shares on the stock market) as the newly opened opportunities will outweigh businesses lost as a result of growing pessimism before 1 July 1997.

Taiwan will keep on searching for international acknowledgement, backing its efforts with its robust and outward-looking economy. Singapore's aspirations to become a regional hub for information, telecommunications, finance, research and education, based on its environment-centred and human-friendly development scheme, are also promising elements for future contacts. Vietnam with its transitory economy and still existing reminiscences of good relations with Hungary is perhaps one of our best chances, while the other ASEAN members, particularly the most populous ones, rich in raw materials and/or fuels, would no doubt have appreciated it if Hungary had intensified its endeavour to seek closer relations with them at the time of their financial difficulties. Bad times go by anyway and what remains is their well-formulated social and economic development plans offering excellent opportunities for partnership. The two Koreas, doomed to reunite in the not too distant future, could perhaps utilize the mediation of a small, far-away country which, at the same time, has been internationally praised for successfully changing its political and economic systems.

Hungary's recently acquired membership in the OECD, after a decade and a half with the World Bank and IMF, and its successfully accomplished stabilization programme, has rightly taken it to the entrance doors of NATO and the EU. Thus, reaching a second stage in its transition, or, if you will, modernization process, has also given a new impetus to private companies to set up their representation and start new businesses there. After their first visit to the region in 1990, for example, it took Keidanren, the Federation of Economic Organizations in Japan, seven years to send another delegation of top Japanese business leaders to Hungary as a part of their business trip to Central and Eastern Europe.

The group headed by Shoichiro Toyoda, Chairman of Keidanren and Toyota Motor Corporation, and many of the twelve vice chairmen of the extremely influential organization had, no doubt, been closely watched by their Japanese colleagues back home, thus creating new interest in this part of the world. Hirotaro Higuchi, Chairman of Asahi Breweries Ltd., Japan's second largest brewery, and formerly Vice President of Sumitomo Bank, as also part of the delegation, said in an interview that 'Hungary is now regarded as a country where you can invest'.[5] He also agreed that doubling the USD 500 million-worth stock of Japanese FDI in Hungary within three years was a realistic forecast. Needless to say, evaluations like that of *The Economist* declaring Hungary as the single country in its region to be on the safe side concerning its currency, can contribute a lot to the image of a country.[6] It is well worth pointing out here that a market with a stabilized economy and entering a sustainable growth pattern can equally attract the attention of Western European and Asian businessmen. Therefore, even the chance of some joint ventures by these in Hungary might come to the fore in the years to come.

I, for one, could easily visualize that at a later date, ASEM members would not insist on holding their meetings in cities of member countries only. Budapest, much experienced in hosting global and regional conferences at all levels, could well be their first choice for a change.

Hungary could, in fact, become a regional centre for tourism, and banking and finance, two sectors of growing international importance from the point of view of the Far Eastern countries, as well. Our comparative and hopefully also competitive advantages in these fields can be defined as follows:

a) in tourism

Apart from the geographic, cultural and historical conditions, all making Hungary, and especially Budapest, an ideal site for tourism, contributions worth pointing out are:

* the one-year-old direct air connection between Bangkok and Budapest;
* the high and continuously growing number of Japanese tourists who, for the time-being, arrive mostly in the summer by charter flights;
* the rapid increase in the number of language schools and their students for Far Eastern languages;
* our traditional relationship with the Western and the Eastern world;
* the closeness of Prague and Vienna, thus extending our 'offer' to include these cities on the same tour (the latter city accessible by air, super-express, hovercraft on the Danube, or cars on highways);
* still existing 'official' and informal business connections with the former republics of the Soviet Union, based on language abilities as well;
* a fairly extensive number of Far Eastern (mainly Chinese) restaurants;
* networks of hotels, pensions and country inns.

b) in banking and finance

As a general reference, it is worth noting that roughly fifty per cent of all foreign direct investments arriving in Central and Eastern Europe landed in Hungary. In addition, one should bear in mind that:
* the Budapest Stock Exchange has been accepted as one of the most dynamically developing markets, yet run on a stable basis;
* the Hungarian banking sector is relatively developed, the privatization process of which will soon be completed;
* Hungary has internationally renowned former and newer experts in banking and finance, and top-level practitioners and professors in these domains;
* the Hungarian forint has convertibility, and its depreciation is slowing down;
* the country is in a reliable debtor's position, also reflected by the upgrading of our risk rating by Moody's and other international agencies;
* our economic policies have the long-term endeavour of cutting down the level of domestic taxes; and, of course,
* the Hungarian economy is on the rise.

Apart from these 'practical' arguments, we can also mention three more general points.

Hungary, on the basis of its wide network of international relations and increasingly heterogeneous population, is a melting pot, albeit much smaller than the US. The blending of people, ideas and information holds promise of well-known advantages, and makes the country automatically more open, receptive and adaptable to proposals and forms of cooperation no matter how far away their places of origin may be. It is in this context that one should strongly consider the success of the Chinese community which has chosen to settle in Hungary.

Just as a mirror to the previous argument, Hungarians can be found all over the world, thus the 'Hungarian connection' can mean a wide international presence for our partners. In this respect it is well worth pointing out, perhaps at no risk of being taken as an immodest proposition, that representatives of top-level intellectuals from Hungary have acquired international respect in the sciences. Ede Teller, Janos Neumann, Eugene Wigner, Denis Gabor, Albert Szentgyorgyi, Lord Balogh, Lord Kaldor, and Janos Kornai might be the names best known abroad.

Following our change to a free market economy, and the gaining ground of small businesses, characteristics like working hard and having entrepreneurial and risk-taking attitudes, most often associated with Chinese or more generally with people in the Far East, are now simultaneously coming to the fore and are deepening in Hungary as well. This is easy to understand, since these characteristics are not new to us either; they were simply pushed into the background for more than forty years after World War II.

ASIA AND EASTERN EUROPE: MORE DIRECT CONTACTS

It is a must to understand that mediators can only play a temporary role in the international arena. Sooner or later they will either be left out or fully incorporated. Therefore, the Central Eastern European countries should not aim at such a role, but do their best to establish as many direct contacts with Asia as possible. In order to do so they will have to strengthen, first within themselves and then in their foreign policy statements, the view that the Euro-Atlantic orientation does not mean a closed, bloc-type approach. As a matter of fact, the more balanced system of international relations they have, the more welcome they will be by the outside world. Should they decide to go ahead with their diversification efforts, the often-declared 'open regionalism' of Far Eastern countries might come in very handy.

Top-level heads of states or intergovernmental visits do play an essential role in catching the eye of the men in the street and, to a lesser degree, businessmen too. Yet, follow-up actions often seem to lack the same initiative. Coordination of such 'moves' is also crucial, so that negotiations should not be starting from scratch every time. Business orientation, getting down to facts, in today's world is not considered impolite or pushy. When doing so, however, one has to be aware of realities on both sides. A clear-cut view of what we can offer and what we would like to achieve is absolutely necessary. In order to be in a position to carry out talks effectively and efficiently, preliminary information gathering and market research cannot be dispensed with. To that end, local representation can make the biggest contribution.

Judging by the experience of Hungary, embassies and commercial offices are best run when they are combined, thus avoiding redundancies and, let us be frank and self-critical, jealousy. Nevertheless, overly strict principles and a mechanical way of following such principles might prove counterproductive as well. Thus, the best policy seems to be to take decisions on a case-by-case basis, which might give room for a few extra trade representations in countries (or markets!) big enough to be served more intensively. Giving up embassies like we did in the Philippines a few years ago for short-term considerations (i.e. economizing on our finances) might be rushed judgements for which we shall have to pay twice when we decide to go back there.

It is very reassuring to note how the teaching of Asian languages, especially Japanese, Chinese, and Korean, is on the rise in Hungary. Books on and courses in Asian management have also appeared on the market. Equally important is that information on Asian cultures is also being disseminated at an increasing rate. This is done not only on a scholarly level, but amongst laymen as well. Friendship societies, business clubs, and information bulletins all do their part, not to mention the embassies, trade offices and other representatives of Asian countries. Media coverage from daily news to regular business programmes, from detailed analyses to occasional supplements in journals and even daily papers do create a sound basis for keeping the issue in the air. Word-of-mouth information, following the rise in the number of tourists visiting each other's regions is also very beneficial, not to mention the success stories emerging from each other's markets.

It is, of course, always the first steps which are the most difficult to take. But in our case it is rather the second and the third steps that are missing. We should, perhaps, give more thought to facts relating to deep-rooted elements of 'Asian values' like stability, long-lasting personal contacts, precision and utmost care in information gathering, company spirit, group orientedness, diligence, frugality and puritanism, and last but not least a strong attraction to good quality. When conducting business, reliability and prompt reactions even if asking for patience, are absolute musts. We should not expect big deals right away. First, we shall have to prove our abilities by repeatedly performing well in smaller contracts. It will not be easy but definitely rewarding, not only in the bilateral context, because the efforts we shall make will simultaneously put us into the training ground without which no international success is imaginable. Thus the Asian connection might not be the end in itself, but the means towards it. We still have a long way to go.

Notes

1. 'A Partnership of Imbalance: Changes in the Japan-European Relations'. University of Tokyo, Institute of Social Science, *Occasional Papers in Capitalist Economies and International Relations* 9, March 1995, pp. 1-2.
2. 'Sharing Asia's Dynamism: Asian Direct Investment in the European Union'. UNCTAD/ITE/IIT/1, 1997, p. 37.
3. The former share of the Soviet Union and the other Comecon countries in both exports and imports was almost completely taken over by Western Europe, the latter now representing nearly 80 per cent of their total turnover.
4. To illustrate the minuscule character of these investments on a wider scale, it is worth pointing out that the No. 1 Far Eastern investors, Japan's FDI stock in Central *and* Eastern Europe, including the Commonwealth of Independent States, represented approximately 0.1 per cent of its total at the end of 1995. ('Sharing Asia's Dynamism: Asian Direct Investment in the European Union'. UNCTAD/ITE/IIT/1, 1997, p. 20.)
5. *Budapest Business Journal*, 20-26 October 1997, pp. 18-19.
6. *The Economist*, 18 October 1997, p. 91.

CONNECTING ASEM TO THE GLOBAL INFORMATION SOCIETY: THE MOVING SCENE

CÉSAR DE PRADO YEPES

We have recently entered into an era of rapid technological change characterized by almost instant mobility of information around many parts of the world. New decentralized and networked structures of more powerful hardware and software are driving the changes towards what we may call an evolving Global Information Society (GIS). To understand better the economic, political, and other social implications, many private and public actors have already started to take action and engage in dialogue, the Asia-Europe Meeting (ASEM) process being a potentially significant link in the increasingly global process.

This article starts by recalling ASEM developments since its first gathering in March 1996 from a GIS perspective. It then reviews a number of activities between Europe and various Asian countries in the field of information and communication technologies, while arguing for a continuing flexible approach to incorporate ASEM to the GIS. The last part of the article presents more specific suggestions to achieve that goal, suggesting a more transparent and free environment in which private actors may better succeed in bringing Asia and Europe closer together.

ASEM 1 TO ASEM 2

The spontaneity among 15+1 European and 10 East and Southeast Asian leaders participating in the first ASEM that took place in Bangkok, led to a remarkable series of follow-up activities, not disconnected from more GIS developments. At the most general level, economic issues were analysed and discussed in various ways. Ministers and senior officials of foreign affairs, economy and finance have met several times in the past two years to discuss enhancement and liberalization of trade and investment in goods and services, and harmonization and simplification of customs procedures.

There have also been plans to facilitate trade in priority areas, and studies of economic synergy mentioning sectors like telecommunications and consumer electronics. A proposal to connect railroad infrastructures between Europe and Asia has been studied, and the importance to secure infrastructure financing has been raised in business gatherings. In several other groups there have been discussions on the possibilities to exchange technology, generally promote investment, and facilitate the adoption of more common standards and frameworks to protect intellectual property rights.

More specifically concerned with the GIS, a workshop has addressed the future of electronic media, and several initiatives to profit from the Internet to foster particular aspects of the evolving Asia-Europe relationship are now ongoing. They complement the ASEM cultural and social follow-up events that have a crucial, longer-term projection. An Asia-Europe Foundation has been established next to the APEC Secretariat in Singapore with the general aim of promoting exchanges between think-tanks, peoples and cultural groups.

Another important, although lateral initiative was the creation of a network of think-tanks working to facilitate cooperation among policy specialists and address the future of Asia-Europe relations. A high-level Vision Group has been envisioned to come to light after ASEM 2. And while young leaders have started to meet on an annual basis, university exchanges now being developed should allow academics and other future leaders to meet and learn from each other more often.

Quickly building on the first ASEM, these meetings and actions have been characterized by openness and flexibility, and thus may easily complement the existing and growing plethora of GIS-related relations between Europe and Asia. Their variety reflects the diversity within and between both regions, something that ASEM cannot neglect. On one side, there is a 'European' mosaic half-way integrated geographically or in various areas for the first time in history, in which member states share competencies on external relations with the European Commission and linked institutions. On the other, there is an array of East and Southeast 'Asian' nations and cultures of different sizes and degrees of development, which still do not share a common political, economic, or cultural reality, despite various political gatherings at the regional level, the growing Japanese or overseas Chinese transnational economic networks now facing a common regional crisis, or the recent discourses on Asian values aired in the media.

CURRENT CONNECTIONS BETWEEN EUROPE AND ASIA

The great regional diversities in both Europe and Asia are thus reflected in their current interregional exchanges, usually arranged on a bilateral basis. The most comprehensive of all the relations has been that of the European Union and Japan, although bilateral links with Korea, China and ASEAN countries are rapidly growing in intensity, especially in GIS sectors.

Europe-Japan relations reflect many common concerns for growing and mutually beneficial economic relations. In the field of communications, regulatory issues are now very important since both the EU and Japan are undergoing parallel processes of liberalizing and restructuring domestically, while at the same time trying to comply with its global commitments in the frame of trade in basic telecommunication services and trade of information equipment reached in the World Trade Organization in 1997.

In the near future, both partners may need to jointly help resolve important issues like competition rules, protection of intellectual property rights in electronic commerce or the mutual recognition of authorities testing and certifying tradable goods and services. Competition issues in the provision of telecommunication services is especially important now that former telecommunication and media monopolies in both Europe and Japan are being transformed and exposed to greater domestic and international competition.

Having for some years been slow to computerize the country, nowadays both Japanese private and public sectors are investing heavily to put in place the nation's Vision 2000 plans to install systems of widespread broad-band communications as soon as possible within the next decade. This entails, at the same time, efforts to aid domestic developments in technologies promoting commerce in electronic services, the next frontier for Japanese large (and new small) multinationals, which have already developed advanced software for export credit and payment systems, encryption and authentication technologies, and other electronic money systems. Yet, since Japan's debt-ridden banks lack some of the sophisticated financial services available in Europe, there could be many areas of mutual benefit for companies linking Europe and Japan.

This would complement the existing corporate links in growing sectors like mobile telephony, and this may prompt even stronger contacts among public officials meeting bilaterally and multilaterally, including the WTO, OECD and ASEM processes. This is also happening with South Korea, a country that in various economic and regulatory aspects resembles Japan.

Relations between Europe and Korea are nowadays broadly based, encompassing trade, economic cooperation and political dialogue. In 1996, both partners concluded a Framework Agreement on Trade and Cooperation and, in 1997, a more specific accord on Telecommunications Procurement, this being important for the future since both Europe and Korea are producers and consumers of high-technology computer components and telecommunication equipment. At the same, provided that Korea quickly restructures to re-establish its financial credibility, there could be increasing collaboration in other important sectors like software or space technologies, which Korea considers important for its development.

Not only are relations between Europe and Korea becoming important, they may also gain increasing attention since Korea seems eager to play an important role in the international political scene. It is now an active member of WTO, OECD and other multilateral forums like APEC, for which it hosts the Asia Pacific Information Infrastructure Cooperation Center. The third ASEM meeting, gathering in Seoul in the year 2000, may be an excellent occasion for Korea to show its progress in linking with Europe and other Asian partners to the fast lane of the GIS as presented in its 1997 Informatization White Paper.

While Europe's relations with Korea and Japan are important and strengthening, its relations with China are also quickly growing to reflect its new international projection. Since the country of 1.2 billion people let several big cities and coastal areas lead its export-led economic progress, China's increasing bilateral trade relationship with Europe traditionally was paralleled with various scientific and technological cooperation projects, as well as selected joint ventures aiming to aid China's domestic development projects. These include the SPARK programme on rural telephony, TORCH in telecommunications, or the better-known Golden Bridge infrastructure project, the main one of a number of Golden Projects aiming at the informatization of China using advanced fibre-optic and satellite technologies.

This bilateral relationship has led to the adoption by China of several European technologies, including mobile telephony and audio-visual broadcasting. Increasing links in GIS sectors should be reflected in a European Communication being adopted in 1998. Since the vast interior areas of China are still quite underdeveloped, better use of wireless and space technologies could be an area of mutual interest to explore not only bilaterally, but also within an ASEM context, given the wide physical separation between both regions.

However, these public efforts would often require the involvement of private consortia from all over the world. An increasing domestic development in telecommunications may be coupled with a progressive acceptance of direct investment rules set out in the WTO, thus bringing China closer to joining the organization. Thus, ASEM could be a good opportunity for China to advance in a more global direction.

While Europe's political relations with East Asian countries are predominantly conducted on a bilateral level, those with Southeast Asia are increasingly carried out on an interregional basis, although companies still prefer to link to the more promising projects to develop national information societies. Special attention is merited by Singapore's IT2000 master plan, which profits heavily from information technologies to develop and consolidate the island-state as a regional and global economic hub. Its domestically-oriented Singapore One (One Network for Everyone) project will allow a high-level of interactive multimedia applications and services to a population that already enjoys excellent telecommunication infrastructures. Singapore, building upon its well-conceived regional hub position, will surely continue to develop its networks in multilateral forums including ASEM, APEC and the WTO. Yet, its stability as networks' hub is very dependent on the advance of the region as a whole, which is still far from being consolidated.

As within ASEAN, Malaysia, Thailand and Indonesia have also placed high hopes in information and communication sectors for their medium-term development, and have not scaled them back despite the financial crisis that has hit the region since late 1997. Malaysia's original plans for a Multimedia Super Corridor envisions a 40 kilometre-long area spanning to the sea from the present capital, Kuala Lumpur, which will include a new administrative capital, an intelligent city, two telesuburbs, a technology park, a multimedia university, and an intellectual property protection park. In the meantime, Thailand's emphasis on new technologies lies in the promotion of a software park, and the interconnection of the country's governmental and school systems. Although Indonesia's far-reaching Nusantara-21 project expects to connect by cable and satellite the 27 provincial capitals of the country, its plans may be harder to realize given the political difficulties compounding the financial crisis originating in 1997.

The Philippines, Brunei and Vietnam are the other ASEAN countries participating in the ASEM process since the beginning. Although they are less advanced in GIS sectors, as members of ASEAN they hope to contribute to building a working regional grouping in many areas, including telecommunications. For some time now, ASEAN Telecommunications Regulators have been meeting regularly to engage in dialogue, although without much progress. As in 1992, ASEAN countries signed the Singapore Declaration expressing the desire to jointly promote a modern communications infrastructure network, an Action Plan has been elaborated and, in early 1998, senior officials met for the first time to discuss concrete telecommunication projects.

A key element for ASEAN's hopes of economic integration are placed in the creation of a regional free trade association coordinated in the Jakarta-based ASEAN Secretariat. While its mission and profile are still modest, it is growing partly due to an institutional development programme of cooperation with the European Commission, which shows its experience in managing various issue areas, including communication, information, standards and technical barriers to trade. This may well be the focus by which the European Union and ASEAN could foster dialogue on various aspects of the information society, as the recent communication for Creating a New Dynamic in EU-ASEAN Relations demands.

While the issue of Myanmar's membership in ASEAN poses a strain on the political relations, there are other mechanisms for dialogue and cooperation between both regions to supplement the links among private actors. The first roundtable of EU and ASEAN industrialists met in Jakarta in late 1997 to discuss the conditions of industrial and technological cooperation, as well as the challenges of the GIS. The European Union's framework programmes in research and development are conditionally open to other countries, with Asian countries occasionally participating. Its fifth quadrennial programme, stressing converging information and communication technologies will increase, from 1999, its emphasis on international cooperation.

At a broader level, and more specifically concentrating on the GIS, the European Union adopted in 1997 a communication concerning its role in the information society and general world development. The communication calls for a strategy to achieve better coherence of the various existing international cooperation instruments, and presents various courses of action including awareness raising and fostering of dialogue, supporting the establishment of a regulatory framework, making use of available financial instruments, promoting the interconnectability of networks and inter-operability of services, launching pilot projects to demonstrate specific benefits, ensuring cooperation with industry and provision of necessary human resources, and pursuing basic research and development interconnection of research networks.

The actions may be modulated according to particular geographical regions. For developing countries in South and Southeast Asia, the European Union will be advancing in the near future a Europe-Asia Cooperation Programme in the Application of Information and Communication Technology. This Asia IT&C programme would utilize European technological and legislative experience relevant to the interests of the countries involved. For that, it would finance projects, address regulatory cooperation including the deregulation of telecommunication services, as well as the protection and management of intellectual property rights and the establishment of standards. Asia IT&C would also address trade barriers in general, as well as various agreements in information technology. In other words, it could help promote the interconnection and inter-operation between Europe and large parts of Asia for which it will establish a programme management office with two sections, one based at the EC in Brussels, and the other in Asia.

Seeing the variety of relations between both sides of the ASEM process regions, it seems unwise to press for an institutionalized interregional framework to address all the common needs within the GIS. It would risk current advances, and it could also stop addressing properly the variety of actions required to facilitate a truly global information regime for a more general benefit. Yet, the ASEM process can be beneficial in this respect if all members promote useful information exchanges to gain a better overview of the many and diverse developments taking place at a more global level. Let's now look at the main trends.

GLOBAL CONNECTIONS

The GIS is formed of many local developments. Yet, it increasingly requires global awareness and, occasionally, coordination among the various actors involved. Various public institutions, with diverse possibilities of action and often overlapping mandates, have been for some time both cooperating and competing in providing solutions. Nowadays, they are also aided and challenged by a plethora of private forums usually springing from collaborative efforts in scientific and technological research of multinational corporations.

The oldest and most global of all relevant institutions is the International Telecommunications Union (ITU). Established in 1865 to ensure common standards for the interconnectivity and inter-operability of telegraph traffic, the ITU has been, since 1947, part of the United Nations system and has taken responsibility for the various new technologies that have been developing, including fixed wire telephony, radio, television, satellite communications and mobile telephony. It is nowadays trying to play a role in the standardization of all types of global information infrastructures. This requires reaching agreements on network transport systems and user interfaces, as well as properly allocating the scarce air and space resources (spectrum and orbital lots), required to actualize foreseen development in mobile and fixed network telephony, as well as broadcast applications.

Its various working groups are working hard to give useful input to the policy and decision bodies of the ITU; its global institutional nature makes it difficult to react on time to rapid technology changes. The organization's 1998 Plenipotentiary Conference will try to solve some of the problems it faces. Perhaps the new leadership can better address current global needs. Two Asian candidates, one from Japan and the other from Indonesia, have been suggested for that job.

Due to the convergence of technologies involved in the GIS, the role of the ITU has been partially converging with those of the International Organization for Standardization (ISO) and the International Electrotechnical Commission (IEC), both also under the United Nations, and trying to redefine their roles while quickening their procedures. If they cannot transform themselves, they may be relinquishing their prerogatives to other groups. Among them, one sees a greater prominence of regional standardization bodies. The main one, based in southern France, is the European Telecommunications Standardization Institute (ETSI). While open to members from all over the world, it has already standardized important technologies produced by mainly European companies with international projection. Asia has no similar counterparts yet. Under the leadership of Japan, however, Asian countries may in the coming years form ATSI, a regional body promoting the technologies of the region's companies. This may overlap with the regional free trade area envisioned by ASEAN countries for the next decade.

Still, many new technologies are conceived and promoted by a small group of private companies, often of global reach. They may be open or restricted consortia, but they always try to quickly go their own way into the market if the technical specifications agreed among themselves are not sanctioned by public standardization institutions like ETSI or ITU. This attitude often conflicts with parallel technological developments, which to some is a sign of healthy market competition, and to others an expression of wasteful lack of coordination among standardization bodies.

Given the perhaps chaotic and inefficient situation in standardizing technical issues, a number of global collaboration ideas and projects would like to put some order. Many of them are being listed in the server of the Global Collaborations virtual roundtable (http://www.globalcollaboration.org), formed out of a joint ISO/IEC working group on the Global Information Infrastructure. Yet, also a number of non-technical issues are increasingly in need of standardization to allow a secure and efficient development of the GIS.

For that far-reaching objective, the European Commissioner in charge of standards and information society, Martin Bangemann, announced in 1997 that he would like to see an International Charter become a platform to address from all sides the multiple issues affecting evolving global communications. While the United States government may favour a different approach, some Asian countries seem to think that the proposal merits closer attention. There might be then a way for ASEM countries to exchange views on this important topic.

The reason behind this urgent need is the current prospects of electronic commerce, that is, a series of old and new technologies enabling faster international procurement of physical goods, as well as instantaneous trade in intangible services. These may be music or video on demand, health and education applications, or trade in money and financial services. While networks of companies and research centres are already using some of these technologies among themselves, less entrepreneurial users, including residential users and public institutions, might wait to have more secure systems of intellectual property rights, taxation, electronic payments, or content regulation.

Due to the newness of the problems and global economic and legal diversity, finding widespread consensus will not be easy. For that, there are issues where European and Asian countries may want to start looking closely together at issues like intellectual property rights or content regulation to bridge their differences and join in reaching a global solution. While at the European Union level there are already a number of legal advances in various issues, in Asia only Japan's Ministry of International Trade and Industry has presented internationally a first concrete initiative to promote electronic commerce. In many other Asian countries the need to address the challenges of electronic commerce is only now becoming prominent. As more countries raise their concerns, unilateral or bilateral proposals would need the sanction of more global bodies.

The World Intellectual Property Organization is another United Nations institution that will play an important subsidiary role, since it established a new framework convention for intellectual property rights in 1996. More recently, the Paris-based Organization for Economic Cooperation and Development, grouping most developed economies including Japan and Korea in Asia, is studying the issue to present useful policy recommendations. Also based in Paris, and looking for a leading role, is the International Chamber of Commerce. Less clear are the potential contributions of other organizations like the United Nations Educational, Scientific and Cultural Organization, whose mandate is vague for the present needs.

In addition, the United States-based Internet Society and the World Wide Web Consortium are among the non-governmental open forums that are also increasingly important in the regulation of the GIS. They have been leading in the definition of the Internet architecture and creation of technical standards at various levels of technology. Another activity coordinated by the Internet Society was the polemic creation in 1997 of generic top-level Internet domain names, a scarce resource lacking geographical specificity. Existing domains (com, edu, net, gov, org, mil, int) are being joined by store, nom, firm, web, info, rec, and arts. This solution is considered by various European and Asian countries as disfavourable, so the decision may continue to raise debate in the future and increase Europe-Asia exchanges of opinions.

In the meantime, the World Trade Organization may be the best-suited multilateral organization to address some of the broader pressing concerns. While not truly global (China and Russia are negotiating their entry), most of its members were, in 1997, able to reach substantial agreements in the international trade of information technology equipment, and in basic telecommunications and financial services. While their implementation is only now starting, the WTO has monitoring and still credible enforcement mechanisms that other international organizations lack. The agreements do not directly address the need to regulate global electronic commerce.

Yet, while the WTO prepares for a new round of negotiations starting not later than the year 2000, it may in the meantime prove flexible enough to address trade issues affected by electronic technologies though the combination of various existing mechanisms. One of them is the provision for Trade Related Aspects of Intellectual Property Rights. Another one allows to reach generic and specific mutual recognition agreements in the testing and certification of products, so the interfaces of electronic commerce might be addressed that way, leaving the technical aspects to private-led groups. This and other non-tariff trade barriers can be addressed in various committees. They will have to be flexible and open to any possibility as all the actors involved in the GIS find an acceptable mixture of regulatory solutions to their common concerns - flexible and imaginative - as the process from the first to the second ASEM has been.

THE ASEM LINK TO THE FUTURE

The lack of structure of the first ASEM in 1996 quickly produced surprise breakthroughs as shown earlier in this article. The lack of structure of the GIS has also produced good results for innovative companies, and likewise for an increasing number of less nimble enterprises quickly adapting to the new situation. While some turmoil is bound to recur after the financial crisis in several Asian countries due to the quick global mobility of capital, the main risks for an improved GIS are trying to stop or heavily distort the flexibility of the process. Since most efforts may easily fail, among the actions the public sector cannot forget is the nurturing of widespread physical infrastructures and human resources capable to thrive in a more interconnected world.

European and Asian countries may then see the interest in promoting the interconnection of basic infrastructures across both regions. Although increasing, the direct dedicated facilities between them may not be sufficient for the needs of interactive multimedia applications that are being developed now. While a number of regional and global satellite projects are being developed, and the number of terrestrial and submarine cables linking Europe and Asia is increasing, today's Internet packet-switched traffic, which travels unmeasured around the world searching the fastest route to its destination, usually finds its way through the United States when flowing back and forth between Europe and Asia.

If both continents want to communicate better and more cheaply, the ASEM process should increase its dialogues with many other countries in Eastern Europe, Western and Central Asia, the Mediterranean Sea and the Indian Ocean, which are now trying to find ways to upgrade their communication systems. Providing secure investments for infrastructure, as well as promoting the open standards and interconnections among less developed areas should be considered by European and Asian public and private bodies, maybe with the collaboration of other multilateral institutions. While this may not be easy, this action would be a far-reaching sign that ASEM is open to find more global solutions to common concerns.

To develop better human resources, governments may need to educate and interconnect people of various age levels. Even in industrialized countries, adult workers are generally not yet directly exposed to the new technologies, so new efforts to retrain them may be necessary. Important as this point is, more crucial is the need to train the newer generations to adapt quickly to the GIS.

At the domestic level, most European countries and some countries in Asia have plans to use Internet technologies in schools early next decade. Between both regions, existing and planned cooperation in the social and cultural fields involving young leaders or students may want to benefit from the study and use of many GIS aspects. At the scientific level, both Europe and East Asia are nowadays creating faster, virtual, regional research networks that could be interconnected in the near future. Yet, this type of arrangement needs to be enhanced and sustained to keep up with the continuously upgrading technological developments.

Not only capital investments are required to lay the foundations of the GIS however. Cheaper but bolder decisions are needed, including making useful information generally accessible. Governments and administrations of both Europe and Asia, not always fully transparent in their objectives and actions, are increasing their public awareness campaigns as well as redesigning their policies concerning public access to non-confidential information. Since new Internet technologies are extremely simple tools for a new kind of democracy, maybe both regions could decide to cast aside the misleading debate of Asian versus Western types of values to jointly help create better forms of global development and governance.

This is of course easier said than done, yet some common actions are not intrinsically difficult. A good start may be collaborating in defining statistical methodologies and providing data for monitoring purposes, given the scarcity and lack of reliability of current efforts, including those of the OECD. A special meeting of the then G7 group of industrialized countries hosted in early 1995 by the European Commission in Brussels, agreed on 11 pilot projects to advance the GIS in areas of general interest, including health, culture, education and training, and general information. Among them is the Internet Global Inventory Project (GIP) which provides access to many national activities of an increasing number of countries around the world including the European Union, Japan and Korea. This type of collaborative exercise could then be expanded to incorporate also more specific data and indicators that would allow a better management of the GIS.

While not yet fully multilingual, the GIP is the first collaborative exercise among an increasing number of diverse countries, which could then set a trend in promoting more global multilingual and multicultural Internet collaboration.

The issue of multilingual and multicultural exchanges may be the most difficult of all to address. Trying to standardize cultural expressions has never been easy, and often not desirable. Much better would be to improve the hardware and software interfaces people use to communicate and do business with each other. Electronically, this means for example having multilingual input devices (keyboards), transmission protocols, searching and retrieval engines, and more translation tools for European and Asian languages. In the past, linguistic diversity has been a major source of interaction, although not overcome by many. Yet, with the ongoing advances in software protocols, it is easier than ever to manipulate non-Latin character sets as well as images.

While the GIP has its own website (http://www.gip.int), it is not, for the time being, fully multilingual. It can also be reached through the European Commission Information Society Project Office website located at (http://www.ispo.cec.be). There one may find an increasing amount of information on the activities in information and communication not only in Europe, but also in Japan and other countries. It is part of the main public website of the European Union institutions (http://europa.eu.int), where one could search in various European languages for specialized databases and recent developments of the European Union, including its relations with Asian countries.

Asian countries do not have yet a common website with similar characteristics, although there are a few sites of related interest. The ASEAN Secretariat's website (http://www.asean.or.id) hosts a good amount of information in English concerning many aspects of its regional integration process. Some ministries and public institutions in other Asian countries also have increasing amounts of information in English and other languages. For regional technology issues, one could, for instance, visit the Japan Patent Office website (http://www.ipo-miti.go.jp), although one may also access the on-line databases of the Asian Technology Information Program (http://www.atip. or.jp) and browse into the Japan Information Access Project linked to the New Mexico Japan Center (http://www.nmjc.org/jiap/about.html). These last two websites are backed by the United States, and freely provide or guide one to procure information on relevant Japanese and Asian issues.

A number of other interesting websites are also being developed in Europe or through bilateral collaboration agreements. The EC-Japan Centre for Industrial Cooperation, a joint venture by the European Commission and Japan's Ministry of International Trade and Industry has for some time tried to achieve mutual economic benefit. It now has two mirror sites, one in Japan (http://www.eu.japan.co.jp) and the other in Germany (http://www.gmd. de/EU_Japan).

Of academic interest on Asian and Europe-Asian issues is the website of the Netherlands-based International Institute for Asian Studies (http://iias. Leidenuniv.nl), and for more general interests, the newer website of the

Brussels-based European Institute for Asian Studies (http://www.net7.net/eias/cyberforum) has taken the lead in promoting public policy, social dialogue and economic exchanges between Europe and Asia. Both websites also present useful links to other Internet resources around the world.

These technologies have helped the author of this article to collect many loose materials and understand better the evolving relations between Europe and Asia in a more interconnected world. As more academics use these new means of communication, future editions of the Stocktaking Survey on Asia-Europe Intellectual Exchange in several countries, prepared in 1997 by the Council for Asia-Europe Cooperation, would be radically different. The first results indicated how very little has so far been written on broad policy issues affecting present-day Europe-Asia relations. Since the original idea of ASEM has flourished in parallel to the GIS, future updates of the survey might also be better placed on the web to account for the expected growth in well-informed on-line exchanges between Europe and Asia.

CHALLENGES AND PROBLEM AREAS

GETTING SERIOUS ABOUT ASIA-EUROPE SECURITY COOPERATION

DONG-IK SHIN AND GERALD SEGAL

When Asia and Europe held their first summit in Bangkok in March 1996, little thought had been given to how the relationship might develop in the future. It was agreed in Bangkok that the Asia-Europe Meeting (ASEM) process should continue; future summits were scheduled for London in 1998 and Seoul in 2000. Much to the surprise of most observers, and to a mixed sense of pleasure and concern on the part of Asian and European officials, the ASEM process has sped off in diverse directions. Various initiatives have been undertaken under ASEM auspices, some of which are devoted merely to sustaining the ASEM process, and others of which are designed to develop 'products' to come out of ASEM 2 in London. Unlike the more developed and longer-standing Asia-Pacific Economic Cooperation (APEC) process, the ASEM process explicitly includes political and security - as well as economic - matters. But while there is a great deal of optimism that ASEM can create a serious agenda for economic relations, there is far less detailed thought about its security agenda.[1] As will be argued below, if Europeans and Asians wish to develop a serious and well-rounded relationship, then they can - and must - become much more serious about security cooperation.

It is easy to be cynical about a security dimension to the Asia-Europe relationship. Europeans withdrew from a major and active military role in Pacific Asia decades ago. The United States is the only world superpower and a major player in both Asian and European balances of power. Given these realities, any thinking about security issues in ASEM has to recognize the limits of security cooperation, and the continuing central role of the US. But even within these limits, there is a case to be made that Europeans and Asians need to work more closely together on security issues.

Europeans have as much stake in a stable and prosperous Pacific Asia as the Americans do and arguably both Europeans and Americans have an even greater stake in Pacific Asia than they have in a stable Middle East. Cynics like to suggest that Europe lags behind the US in developing an economic interest in Pacific Asia and that it has no interest in serious security cooperation with

Asians. In recent years, however, Europe's economic relationship with Pacific Asia has caught up with US levels of investment and trade. In the security sphere, Europeans sometimes have different traditions and policies from Americans and will therefore bring different (but not necessarily inferior) ideas to the relationship with the region.

The analysis and argument that follows is designed to contribute to what is admittedly a nascent process of thinking seriously about security in ASEM. Embarking on such a task is motivated by an assumption that neither Europeans nor Asians will take each other as seriously as they should and could if relations are left entirely in the economic domain. Nowadays power and influence require a more full-bodied sense of interests and relations. The transatlantic relationship - which includes economic and security cooperation - is an example of a full-bodied relationship, whereas the APEC model - which only deals with economic issues - is more an example of 'lite' diplomacy.[2] If Europeans wish to be taken seriously in Pacific Asia, they will have to think hard about security questions. If Asians wish to help in keeping their region secure and prosperous, and have an easier time 'managing' the United States, they will have to engage in tough discussions with Europeans about common security interests. This is not a matter of wishful thinking; there is already important evidence of Euro-Asian cooperation in both hard and soft security, and there is a substantial and achievable agenda for future action.

THE SECURITY AGENDA

In an age when the definition of security is hotly contested, this is not the place to offer anything more than a pragmatic understanding of the term for ASEM. What is obvious to policy makers, even if it is not to academic specialists in both Europe and Asia, is that, in an interdependent world, the economic and military dimensions of security cannot be separated. Is supplying energy to booming economies an economic or security issue? Does the presence of a huge trade surplus have security implications for two rival states (for example, China and the United States)? Clearly it makes sense to have a flexible understanding of security in the real world.

HARD SECURITY

Europeans used to be major players in the 'hard security' of Pacific Asia. After the colonial powers withdrew from Asia, however, there was a period of distancing between Asia and Europe. While the US was carving out its sphere of influence, European countries focused on the threat from the former Soviet

Union and how to cooperate with the US. Europe's security ties with Asian countries were relatively weak, although it had traditional interests in the region stemming from historical relations.

When the Cold War ended, there was little left of high-profile, hard European security in Pacific Asia.[3] The UK and France still deployed a small number of forces in the region, partly as residual colonial commitments. European forces exercised with regional allies in the US-led RimPac exercises. Bilateral cooperation among armed forces took place, for example, between the UK and Japan during the 1990s. The most important network involving Europeans was the Five Power Defence Arrangements (FPDA) linking the UK with former colonies in Singapore, Malaysia, Australia and New Zealand. In recent years, Australia has played the leading role in the FPDA, but the UK has reaffirmed its commitment, even after the withdrawal from Hong Kong in June 1997.

Cynics are correct in noting that an important part of the British motive in sustaining the FPDA is the desire to sell arms in Pacific Asia. They are also right to view arms sales as having much to do with economic motives. But weapons transfers are more than just moneymaking ventures: arms transfers have a serious security calculation. When weapons and weapons systems are sold, they often include not only high technology, but also a sustained effort to train soldiers and provide follow-up technology. Transfers include discussions about doctrine and training methods. In many cases, they also include implicit and sometimes explicit transfers of intelligence information.

European countries are often prepared to offer better terms to local states, for example, by allowing Asians more access to classified source codes - and Asians find that competition in the arms market helps make the Americans more willing to satisfy Asian arms requirements. Sometimes the equipment and training provided by Europeans is better suited to the needs of Asia's middle powers than US equipment. European companies have already begun to work well with the main regional Western ally - Australia - in multilateral defence cooperation.

Arms transfers obviously need to be conducted in a way that helps build security and enhance deterrence. Arms transfers motivated by a shortsighted commercial temptation could increase instability by undermining the regional balance of power, but a sensible arms-transfer strategy is vital to building security and enhancing deterrence. Similar calculations applied when the UK and France (like the US) signed defence agreements with Kuwait, Qatar and the United Arab Emirates after having sold large amounts of weapons to these Gulf States. If Europeans are anxious to see Southeast Asians defend themselves in the South China Sea, believe that South Korea should be able to defend itself against North Korea, or think that robust deterrence should be maintained in the

Taiwan Strait, then arms transfers can be powerful and important contributions to hard security.

It is therefore significant that European arms transfers to Pacific Asia have sustained a market share of more than 20 per cent since 1992. The main arms suppliers are the UK, France and Germany, all of whom can provide state-of-the-art equipment and can sustain long-term security relationships. Europeans can expect to expand their market share and thereby extend their role in the region's hard security.

Arms transfers and the details of military-to-military cooperation are obviously not issues to be discussed at the highest ASEM level. Many of the calculations about security interests include an assessment that one or another ASEM member can be a threat to a neighbour. But if the ASEM process is understood as 'variable geometry' - different tasks can be backed by changing coalitions of the ready, willing and able - then certain Europeans and certain Asians may find reasons to work together on hard security. For that reason alone, security issues can and are likely to be raised in the formal ASEM agenda.[4]

Another reason to discuss hard security relates to the possibility of deploying European military assets in Asian zones of tension. Imagine if the United States sought support from allies in breaking a possible blockade in the Taiwan Strait, or in defending South Korea from a North Korean attack. At least some Europeans are likely to heed a US call for allies, much as they did in the 1991 Gulf War. As in the Gulf, Washington would take the lead, but the Europeans would be significant players. It was a well-leaked secret that, during the Taiwan Strait crisis of March 1996, the US consulted more closely with the UK and France about possible contingencies than it did with nearly all states in Asia-Pacific. For Europe, defending a stable Pacific Asia that remains open and connected to the global economy is a vital interest, and one worth defending with military power. The Europeans would be foolish to free ride on the US willingness to defend an open and stable global trading system if a challenge arises in Asia.

SOFT SECURITY WITH A HARD EDGE

If Europeans and Asians are serious about working together on some aspects of hard security, then they should discuss the wider security environment in an ASEM context. Europe and Asia can develop security cooperation by exchanging views on international security and sharing responsibilities on common security issues. Therefore, ASEM needs to undertake a regular and detailed review of political and security situations in both regions. These discussions should include the roles of Asians and Europeans in dealing with issues of regional and global importance. Although direct participation in each other's security is limited, political and diplomatic support can, and probably will, be of greater importance in mutual security cooperation.

One obvious area for closer Euro-Asian cooperation is in confidence-building measures (CBMs). As is clear in the Organization for Security and Cooperation in Europe (OSCE) process, it is useful to establish methods and habits of consultation and cooperation. Asia hopes that Europe will share its experience about the regional operation of CBMs, preventive diplomacy and conflict resolution. In that context, Japan and Korea have participated in OSCE meetings with 'Partner for Cooperation' status. While Europe already has regional institutions - such as the OSCE, NATO and Partnership for Peace - Asia has only the ARF, which is still in its infancy, but is making modest progress in CBMs. The OSCE has been successful in implementing pre-notification of military exercises, 'open-sky' policies and exchanges of military officers. In Asia, however, only ASEAN has had some experience of some CBMs, through bilateral Joint Commission Meetings and multilateral ASEAN meetings. The countries in Northeast Asia have only begun to discuss CBMs through the Northeast Asia Cooperation Dialogue - a semi-official dialogue between the US, China, Russia, Japan and South Korea launched in 1993 - with China's positive participation in the dialogue. Europe's support and cooperation will be important in enabling Asia to generate its own security mechanisms for CBMs and conflict prevention in the region. Since the EU is already a member of both the ARF and ASEM, interregional cooperation on CBMs can be developed without too many complications. European countries can share their experiences with Asian partners through meetings or even via more concrete training, as was explored in the Middle East arms control process.[5]

Confidence-building measures in Europe were developed by a combination of political and military factors over 15-20 years. Europeans are the first to acknowledge just how complex the CBM process can be and how the CBM agenda can easily be over-sold.[6] Accordingly, confidence building in Asia will take time because the region is divided by different cultural, historical, political and economic conditions. Several basic lessons can be learned from the European experiences, however. First, the development of arms control and CBM initiatives is inevitably a highly selective, evolutionary process. Second, positive political developments among neighbours can create conditions for the successful pursuit of CBMs. Third, the most important task of CBMs is to promote transparency and undermine the rationales behind secrecy.[7]

Europeans can be helpful at a practical level in helping Asians work through implementing CBMs. Of special interest are those concerning information and notification of exercises and operations. Such measures might include defence policy publication, enhancing high-level defence contacts and exchanges among defence staff-college and military-training vessels, encouraging compliance with the UN Register of Conventional Arms, and notification of major military exercises. Parallel with the ARF activities on CBMs in the Asia-Pacific region, ASEM could hold working group meetings (or workshops) on promoting transparency and CBMs with more input from all EU members. As in the Middle East case, Europeans can be of value not just in conference rooms, but also in field exercises and detailed operational discussions that explain how such CBMs work. The best form of collaboration would include intensive contacts among military officers working on issues of current concern.

Another area of cooperation to be explored is 'preventive diplomacy'. European countries have undertaken preventive diplomacy and peacemaking efforts to help stop the emergence or escalation of conflicts. Europe's experiences and principles - such as early mediation and the preventive deployment of troops within the OSCE framework - can be valuable to Asia. As a mid-term measure, Asian countries may also want to explore the idea of a regional mechanism for conflict prevention and risk reduction that the OSCE has successfully pioneered for European security.

Peacekeeping operations are likely to be another major and fruitful area for mutual cooperation. European countries have played a leading role in promoting peacekeeping activities in various conflicts and Asian countries are actively expanding their peacekeeping roles. Europeans have already been very active in the peace settlement in Cambodia, where a large UN force was deployed from February 1992-November 1993. Individual European and Asian countries (for example, Malaysia and the UK) already have detailed working relationships in peacekeeping, including the provision of equipment to Asian states, such as Malaysia.

Individual EU states are the largest contributors to the UN's peacekeeping operations budget, providing over one-third of the total contribution and nearly one-third of the total personnel assigned to UN peacekeeping operations. Asian countries - in particular Japan, Malaysia and Korea - have greatly increased their contributions to peacekeeping activities by providing both military personnel and finances. If the United States remains reluctant to put its forces under UN command, peacekeeping operations will become an even more important area where Europeans and Asians can discuss expanding their cooperation at the ASEM level.

Asian and European countries can work together closely within the UN system; they can strengthen UN peacekeeping activities by taking part in the UN Stand-by Arrangements and by becoming Parties to the Convention on the Safety of United Nations and Associated Personnel. ASEM member countries can also promote greater sharing of peacekeeping experience and expertise through training courses on specialized peacekeeping activities; they can foster cooperation among national peacekeeping training centres. Training peacekeeping personnel and providing necessary equipment will be essential for the success of such activities. It is noteworthy that Northern European countries have already hosted peacekeeping training courses for military personnel and civilian staff from Asian countries.[8]

To improve the capabilities of peacekeeping forces, seminars could be held at the ASEM level on European experiences in deploying the NATO-led Peace Implementation Force (IFOR) to Bosnia. Such efforts will build a deeper understanding of peacekeeping operations and find more areas for cooperation between the two regions. Peacekeeping, with its obvious links to those involved in 'harder security', illustrates that the ASEM process can involve security issues in a mature and meaningful manner.

CBMs might accompany introducing a peacekeeping regime. In a region where states are unable or unwilling to negotiate CBMs of their own accord, cooperation in peacekeeping might itself be considered an important measure for confidence building.[9] In this sense, joint peacekeeping activities can provide some Asian countries (notably China, Japan and South Korea) with opportunities to ease suspicions among their neighbours. This type of transparency-enhancing CBM could be a valuable lesson for Asian countries lacking experience in military cooperation.

As Europe and Asia clearly have common goals in creating a climate of peace and prosperity in both regions, non-proliferation and disarmament issues - such as the Nuclear Non-Proliferation Treaty (NPT), Comprehensive Test Ban Treaty, Chemical Weapons Convention, Biological Weapons Convention, Missile Technology Control Regime and International Atomic Energy Agency (IAEA) safeguards - should also be discussed in the global security context. Both Asia and Europe can exchange views, and cooperate on arms control and disarmament in ASEM - as well as in multilateral forums, such as the UN and the Conference on Disarmament. These major initiatives embrace regional security imperatives and therefore discussions on enhancing global regimes have both a global and regional impact.

Although the NPT has been extended indefinitely in the 1995 New York Review and Extension Conference, there remains a risk of nuclear proliferation in the NPT regime. For example, while North Korea claims special status under the NPT, it is unwilling to allow the IAEA to make special inspections at suspicious sites where undeclared reprocessing activities have taken place. Since the non-proliferation regime must keep a careful watch for further cases of actual or potential non-compliance in the world, Asia and Europe have good reason to cooperate through the ASEM process to prevent any secret nuclear development or clandestine nuclear trade, and to strengthen the IAEA's effective safeguard systems.

Europeans, after a slow start, have finally made a serious financial contribution to the Korean Peninsula Economic Development Organization (KEDO), established in March 1995 following the October 1994 US-North Korean nuclear agreement. South Korea and Japan were both keen for Europeans to contribute actively on an issue of key Asian insecurity, but those European states strongly opposed to nuclear power of any sort delayed effective EU action for some time. Seoul, however, kept up a constant campaign to gain a European contribution to KEDO. Tokyo reminded Europe that Asians helped with the post-Chernobyl relief efforts, believing that such matters are of global importance. In the end, the Europeans did make a serious contribution to Asian security and demonstrated that there is a concrete basis for further Euro-Asian cooperation on such soft security issues with hard edges.

UNCONVENTIONAL AND NON-MILITARY SECURITY

Energy security is an important issue which both Asian and European countries can also address within the context of comprehensive security. Asia's emerging energy problem could cause security problems if such high rates of economic growth continue without major changes in the pattern of energy consumption or a reduction in the costs of exploiting energy resources. There is growing, if somewhat over-stated, concern about the potential for severe strains between Asian economic powers. These concerns, especially in Northeast Asia, make nuclear power highly attractive as a major alternative energy source. Japan generates nearly one-third of its electricity from nuclear power, while South Korea gets around 40 per cent.[10] In the APEC process, there have been several high-level meetings among member countries to discuss the impact of increasing demands for various types of energy in the Asia-Pacific.

Peaceful use of nuclear energy may become an important way to resolve the shortage of energy in the region. While Europe has handled civil nuclear energy through the European Atomic Organization (EURATOM) for forty years, Asia is now in the early stage of thinking about establishing a regional mechanism for nuclear energy cooperation. There have been early initiatives by Japanese and other Asian countries to establish a regional body that might be called 'ASIATOM', which might manage some aspects of the huge increase in energy needed in the region. Since there are already significant areas of cooperation between European and Asian countries in the nuclear area, it will be logical to explore further nuclear energy cooperation at the ASEM level.

The potential applicability of EURATOM to Asia needs to be seen in relation to both nuclear non-proliferation and the development of civilian nuclear power. There are similarities and differences in conditions between the two regions. While EURATOM was established systematically after the Second World War, 'ASIATOM', once established, will need to develop gradually, in accordance with rapidly changing local conditions.[11] In Asia, only Northeast

Asian countries and a few other Asian states have actively been developing nuclear power plants; concerns regarding nuclear proliferation therefore remain high, but narrowly focused. Any lessons drawn from the EURATOM model would have to be modified for Asian circumstances. As economic and technical needs alone do not yet justify 'ASIATOM', better understanding of nuclear safety and non-proliferation, and close cooperation for the peaceful use of nuclear energy, could both be promoted at the ASEM level. European experiences such as nuclear waste (spent fuel) management, measures for nuclear safety, and advanced nuclear research and development will be useful for developing nuclear energy cooperation with Asian countries.

A second area of cooperation concerns the security of shipping and freedom of navigation on the high seas. Europe and Asia have an interest in cooperating on this issue because ensuring freedom of navigation is a critical concern for both regions. European countries, especially the UK and France, are keen to improve exchanges with a range of Asian states on protection of open sea-lanes. Europe has a great deal of expertise in cooperating in maritime salvage, search and rescue, and preventing and clearing maritime pollution. Asian countries also have a critical interest in securing free passage, particularly in the Malacca Strait and around the Spratly Islands, to protect their trade routes and natural resources. In particular, Japanese and South Korean industries depend heavily on oil imports from the Middle East through these sea-lanes. Furthermore, the fight against piracy on the high seas, and containing the flow of sea-bound illegal migrants are also issues of concern for both regions.

As well as the major maritime powers (China and Japan), there are an increasing number of medium-size maritime powers in Asia - South Korea, Indonesia and Malaysia, for example - that have extensive maritime interests in the sea in both the strategic and economic sense. For these middle-ranking powers, exchanging experiences and views on these issues will be very useful in promoting maritime cooperation between the two regions. Seminars or workshops on free passage in the Malacca Strait, the Taiwan Strait and the South China Sea could be organized in order to reduce the tension and constitute effective confidence building measures in the region. The implementation of the Exclusive Economic Zone and the UN Convention on the Law of Sea, and the future of the Treaty of Southeast Asia Nuclear-Weapon-Free Zone, signed by ASEAN countries in December 1995, should also be on the ASEM agenda.

Taking an even broader definition of security, food supply problems can also be seen as critical issues for ASEM to discuss. More than 840 million people in the world today do not have adequate access to food, and the situation may deteriorate as the world population increases.[12] While Europeans and East Asians do not face critical food problems, they both have an obligation to the less successful parts of the globe. Some have argued that many Asian states suffer from 'compassion deficit'; a detailed programme of collaboration with Europeans at the ASEM level might help to overcome this perception. Tokyo has already assumed a leading role in humanitarian relief efforts, and many other Asians, as they grow richer, may wish to follow in their footsteps.

Moreover, Europeans and Asians have no reason to be complacent about domestic humanitarian relief problems. In East Asia, there were major operations for Cambodian refugees, Vietnamese boat people and refugees from Myanmar in the 1970s and onwards. In addition, as future possible conflicts might emerge in the region, whether in Indochina, China or on the Korean Peninsula, humanitarian issues may well require major foreign input. Europeans have also faced challenges of this sort in the Balkans and the Caucasus. States in the two regions have much experience to share and collaborative mechanisms to establish. It is clearly advantageous to consider both early-warning mechanisms and methods of response.[13] Various other issues can be identified, including cooperation in fighting the drug trade, international crime and terrorism. But suffice it to say that there is a solid range of important security issues that can be usefully addressed at the ASEM level.

GETTING SERIOUS ABOUT SECURITY COOPERATION IN ASEM

Global economic openness and global security seem to benefit from realistic action at both the regional and interregional level that supports the global systems. 'Open regionalism' is an oxymoron in one sense, but through a system of competitive regional efforts to enhance free trade, regionalism can contribute to a more open global system. Just as the notion of open regionalism has dual meaning, so ASEM has the dual meaning of enhancing openness, and doing so through an implicit constraint on American tendencies to unilateralism.

To achieve these goals, ASEM needs to make progress in economic, political and security terms. Despite its successful start and large scale, it will take a long time before ASEM becomes a fully-fledged and effective institution for interregional cooperation. To do so, ASEM needs to develop a security agenda. As we have suggested, this agenda can be full and fruitful. Some aspects will be best developed in accordance with 'variable geometry' and not include all ASEM members. Some issues are better discussed at a track-two level, at least initially. Others will be mainly handled through official exchanges of information and opinion, leaving harder policy changes for later. The mix of these options is complex; but in the end, there is a real security agenda that includes both hard and soft security. If Europeans and Asians fail to engage in both the process of security discussion and the implementation of certain policies, then before long, ASEM will be judged to have failed to live up to its promise.

Notes

1. See David Camroux and Christian Lechervy, 'Encounter of a Third Kind?': The Inaugural Asia-Europe Meeting of March 1996', *The Pacific Review* 9, no. 3, 1996 and Gerald Segal, 'Thinking Strategically About ASEM: The Subsidiarity Question', *The Pacific Review* 10, no. 1, 1997.
2. 'Lite' powers are reluctant to use military force. The notion is developed in Barry Buzan and Gerald Segal, 'The Rise of 'Lite' Powers', *World Policy Journal* 13, no. 3, Autumn 1996.
3. On this point generally, see Gerald Segal, *Rethinking the Pacific* (Oxford: The Clarendon Press, 1990).
4. François Godement et al., 'Pluses and Minuses in Cooperation Between Europe and Asia', *International Herald Tribune*, 19 November 1996.
5. Marie-France Desjardins, *Rethinking Confidence-Building Measures*, Adelphi Paper 307 (Oxford: Oxford University Press for the IISS, 1996), chapter 1.
6. Peter Jones, 'Maritime Confidence-Building Measures in the Middle East', in: Jill R. Junnola (ed.), *Maritime Confidence-Building in Regions of Tension*, Report 21 (Washington DC: The Henry L. Stimson Center, May 1996).
7. Richard E. Darilek, 'East-West Confidence-Building: Defusing the Cold War in Europe', in: *A Handbook of Confidence-building Measures for Regional Security* (Washington DC: The Henry L. Stimson Center, January 1995), pp. 20-23. See also Fumiaki Takahashi, *What Role for Europe in Asian Affairs?*, Adelphi Paper 276 (London: Brassey's for the IISS, April 1993).
8. Scandinavians - Finland, Sweden, Norway and Denmark - have managed the UN Training Centre to provide training courses for peacekeeping-operations personnel, such as military-observer and logistics courses.
9. Mahbubani, 'The Pacific Impulse', p. 110.
10. Kent Calder, *Asia's Deadly Triangle* (London: Nicholas Brealy, 1996).
11. Tatsujiro Suzuki, 'Lessons from EURATOM for Possible Regional Nuclear Co-operation in the Asia-Pacific Region (ASIATOM)', *Policy Paper* 24 (San Diego, CA: Institute on Global Conflict and Cooperation, University of California at San Diego, August 1996), pp. 29-39.
12. 'Feeding the World', *International Herald Tribune*, 13 November 1996, pp. 8-9, and 16 November 1996, pp. 15-16.
13. According to the German Federal Intelligence Bureau's projection, over 6.5 million North Koreans may escape from North Korea in an emergency. See *Frankfurter Allgemeine Zeitung*, 20 November 1996, p. 6.

COMBATING INTERNATIONAL CORRUPTION: IN SEARCH OF AN EFFECTIVE ROLE FOR ASEM

JONG BUM KIM

Asia's rapid economic growth has been accompanied by economic links with the rest of the world through expanded trade and foreign direct investment. However, Asia's economic link with Europe has lagged behind its link with North America. The first inaugural ASEM in Bangkok, in March 1996, was launched because of the need to provide a forum for linking Asia at various levels. As the second summit in London in 1998 nears, questions arise as to the role ASEM can play in dealing with the important issues of promoting trade and investment between Asia and Europe. Asia and Europe so far have considered ASEM as a venue for developing an infrastructure for facilitating trade and investment. However, ASEM has not engaged in concrete discussions for removing trade and investment barriers. The difficulty lies in the fact that ASEM is not a rule-making body. However, ASEM can play a unique role for developing consensus both in Asia and Europe on many contentious issues before they move to other rule-making bodies. One such issue is combating corruption.

Although it is increasingly recognized that corruption poses barriers to foreign direct investment for developing countries, which need a sustained flow of investment to maintain development, some in Asia as well as in Europe would probably consider fighting corruption in international business relations too sensitive an issue to be discussed at the ASEM level. However, given ASEM's unique status as an organization without hegemony, if such contentious issues like corruption cannot be dealt with at the ASEM level, they probably could not be dealt with in other international organizations like the WTO. Although ASEM is not a rule-making organization such as the WTO or the OECD, it can become a suitable forum for raising consciousness on important and contentious issues like fighting corruption in international business transactions. In other words, ASEM can play a unique role in dealing with common concerns between Asia and Europe and in bringing about consensus on certain issues.

This article begins by looking at the growing importance of FDI (Foreign Direct Investments) in the world economy. This section describes why FDI is playing an increasingly important role in developed as well as developing economies in both Asia and Europe. The second section examines the existing economic relations between Asia and Europe and how they can tap into mutually complementary economic gains by promoting investment between the two regions. The third section shows that combating corruption should be viewed against the background of investment liberalization in multilateral frameworks. Section four then describes the current effort in ASEM to promote trade and investment, followed by section five, which describes the current international efforts to combat corruption. This section argues that combating corruption should be viewed as an effort to provide a level playing field for business. In conclusion, this article argues that ASEM should engage in combating corruption as an important extension of its other investment promotion activities.

FDI'S ROLE IN THE INTERNATIONAL ECONOMY

The most important transformation in the world economy during the last decade has arguably been the rapid expansion of foreign direct investment. Worldwide flow of foreign direct investments began to surge during the mid 1980s. During the 1980s, global FDI increased around 30 per cent annually, more than three times the rate of growth of world exports and four times that of world GDP. The total flow of outward foreign direct investment from industrial economies more than quadrupled from USD 49, 5 billion in 1984 to USD 210 billion in 1991. This outward FDI flow surged again from USD 230 billion in 1994 to USD 318 billion in 1995.[1]

FDI in recent years has been playing an increasingly complementary role to international trade. Multinational manufacturing companies are investing overseas to acquire foreign distribution networks. As the share of services in world trade grows, service-related investment grows faster. Many services require a commercial presence in the foreign country concerned as a precondition for effective market access. As a result, FDI is becoming a necessary managerial extension of domestic operation for gaining access to global markets. Recent FDI is characterized by investment of multinational corporations in their subsidiaries, complementing growing international trade in goods and services, one-third of which consists of exports from multinational corporations. This increasingly complementary role of FDI and trade reflects business globalization taking place over the last decade.

In recent years, developing countries have been receiving an increasing portion of the world's FDI. In 1989, one-fifth of the world's FDI was invested into developing countries versus over 50 per cent at present.[2] This indicates that developing countries' markets are being accessed more and more by the rest of the world through FDI. Notably, Asia's Newly Industrialized Economies

(NIEs) are participating in outward FDI to gain access to markets of developed countries as well as their Asian neighbours. In a globalizing economy, export growth of developing Asian countries cannot be sustained without accompanied growth in FDI.

COMPLEMENTARY ECONOMIC GAINS BETWEEN ASIA AND EUROPE

While economic ties between North America and Asia and between North America and Europe have been strengthening, economic ties between Asia and Europe have remained weak. The thirty-five member countries of ASEM produced 54 per cent of the world's GDP in 1995, of which the EU produced 32 per cent and the remaining 22 per cent by Asian members of ASEM.[3] Although Asia and Europe account for a major portion of the world economy, trade and investment between the two regions have not measured up to the respective sizes of the economies. In 1995, only 14.6 per cent of total imports by Asian members of ASEM originated from the EU. Similarly, in 1995, only 8.8 per cent of total EU imports were from Asian members of ASEM.[4] Hence, the economic size of each region is disproportionate to the region's importance as a trading partner to the other. Therefore, there exists a clear need for tapping into the potential economic gains by promoting trade and investment between Asia and Europe.

This weak economic link between Asia and Europe should be viewed against the backdrop of US emphasis on rebuilding Europe after the Second World War. The war also underscored the need for Europe to promote economic integration in order to avoid another destructive war on the European continent. As Europe deepened its integration, Asia emerged from its colonial past and began to achieve rapid economic growth. The main engine of growth in Asia was export-led policy, which was directed primarily towards the rest of Asia and North America. The combination of European's internal integration and Asia's export-led patterns partly explains the weak economic link between Asia and Europe.

Based on the trend of investment between Asia and Europe, the economic link between the two regions has remained weak during the 1990s despite rapid economic growth in Asia. With regard to ASEAN countries, the share of inward FDI from the EU dropped from 19.7 per cent in 1985 to 13.8 per cent in 1993.[5] In China, the share of inward FDI from the EU declined from 13.6 per cent to 3.8 per cent.[6] The decline in the EU's share of inward FDI to ASEAN countries and China resulted from increased FDI among Asian countries. In contrast to ASEAN and China, the EU's share of FDI to Korea increased from 6.6 per cent to 19.8 per cent during the same period.[7]

Between 1985 and 1987, the share of Korean inward FDI from the EU averaged 7.4 per cent, but increased to 34.8 per cent between 1990 and 1993.[8] The rapid increase in FDI from the EU to Korea is partly explained by the fact that the portion of FDI received from the EU was initially low. In addition, the EU's recognition of Korea as a desirable destination as well as Korea's effort to remove barriers have played significant roles in increasing the share of FDI originating from the EU.

With the exception of Korea, the overall picture of the investment relations between the EU and Asia indicates that they are diverging from closer economic cooperation. Considering its goal of strengthening economic ties between the two regions, ASEM has to develop an infrastructure for a more favourable investment environment. Developing such an environment includes the hard issue of developing a rule-making infrastructure for investment protection, investment liberalization, and dispute settlement. There are also the softer issues of providing government assistance for information exchange, business-to-business exchange, and development of large-scale infrastructure projects. Beyond these, there is the core social and economic issue of combating corruption, which poses a serious barrier to investment. The question is: What role can ASEM play in combating corruption in international and domestic business?

INVESTMENT LIBERALIZATION AND COMBATING CORRUPTION

Providing for a favourable investment environment is important, not only for developed countries, who are the primary sources of FDI, but also for developing countries, whose growth depends on inward FDI by developed countries. Studies indicate that corruption undermines economic growth by reducing private investment.[9] Therefore, developing and developed countries both in Asia and Europe share a common interest in providing a favourable investment climate and dealing with investment barriers such as corruption.

Combating corruption as an investment barrier should be viewed against the backdrop of recent multilateral efforts to develop a multilateral legal framework for a 'national treatment' of investment and 'investment protection'. By granting 'national treatment' to foreign investors, countries promise them that they will be allowed to operate on the same basis as domestic operators. Foreign investors will operate with the expectation that profits and royalties from investment will not be threatened with expropriation.[10]

At the forefront of the most comprehensive multilateral effort to build infrastructure for investment protection, investment liberalization, and dispute settlement, is the OECD's Multilateral Agreement on Investment (MAI). This agreement would be a freestanding international treaty, open to OECD members as well as non-OECD countries willing to abide by its rules.

Complementing OECD's effort, the WTO is also engaged in building a rule-based infrastructure for investment liberalization through the General Agreement on Trade in Services (GATS), which treats the supply of foreign affiliates through local 'commercial presence' as a form of trade in services. GATS, like GATT preceding it, is intended to serve as a framework for the progressive liberalization of services through successive rounds of negotiations.[11]

In addition to the multilateral effort for investment liberalization at the WTO level, regional pacts such as APEC's 'Action Agenda' and the NAFTA (North American Free Trade Agreement) integrate the issues of trade and investment into a single trade agreement. Although conflicts between regional agreements and multilateral agreements still remain, rule-based infrastructure for investment liberalization at the WTO is making steady progress with significant coverage of developing countries.

The primary objective in any agreement on investment is the 'national treatment' of foreign firms, without which corruption in the economy tilts the playing field in favour of domestic firms. If corruption in the domestic market is tolerated, domestic firms, which are more familiar with the corrupt practices of the local market, will have an advantage over foreign firms. In light of the adverse economic consequences of corruption, various international organizations such as the International Chamber of Commerce (ICC) have put forth declarations against corruption in business, such as the 1997 report on 'Extortion and Bribe in Business Transactions'. This was a very ambitious declaration, which even called for an ICC panel to consider allegations of infringement upon the rules of conduct. In response to a wave of bribery scandals in the 1990s, the ICC strengthened its earlier report by calling for governments to implement the May 1994 OECD recommendation calling for governments to make 'effective efforts' in combating corruption. Aided by efforts in other organizations, the OECD adopted a new and strengthened recommendation in 1997, calling for member countries to criminalize bribery of foreign public officials in an effective and coordinated manner by 1 April 1998. In addition, the OECD decided to open negotiations on an international convention to criminalize bribery.[12]

The result of following the OECD recommendations and joining the OECD convention would be twofold. Firstly, firms from an OECD country carrying out this recommendation will be effectively denied national treatment by a host country if the host country tolerates corruption in its domestic market. Secondly, firms from non-OECD members, which tolerate international bribery, will have an advantage over firms from OECD countries. In both cases, corruption undermines a level playing field in the market. Therefore, OECD efforts will be hurt without simultaneous attempts to fight domestic corruption and participation by non-member countries.

A recent empirical finding has shown corruption to be equivalent to taxes on investment, in effect reducing inward FDI. An increase in the corruption level from that of Singapore to that of Mexico is found to be equivalent to raising the tax rate on investment by over 20 per cent.[13] Therefore, tolerating corruption in the host country of FDI results in an inhospitable environment for FDI. In addition, by tolerating corruption by their firms operating in foreign markets, governments undermine the level playing field for investment in the foreign country, consequently damaging that country's investment climate.

ASEM'S ROLE IN TRADE AND INVESTMENT PROMOTION

Since the inaugural ASEM summit in Bangkok in 1996, ASEM has been active in proposing and holding various meetings for investment promotion between Asia and Europe. At the most senior level, ASEM's Economic Ministers Meeting (EMM) was first held in Japan, in September 1997, to discuss economic relations, including trade and investment liberalization, between the two regions. As a working-level meeting, the Senior Official's Meeting on Trade and Investment is drafting the Trade Facilitation Action Plan (TFAP). Korea and the Philippines have drawn up a draft of the TFAP, reflecting Asia's position. In drafting this TFAP, Asian members of ASEM opposed early discussions of trade-related environmental issues, fearing protectionist motives behind raising environmental concerns about products in Asia's developing countries.

At the private level, the Asia-Europe Business Forum held its first meeting in France in October 1996. Participants of the first meeting adopted a recommendation to build a strong economic infrastructure between Asia and Europe. The Business Forum's second meeting is scheduled to be held in November 1997 to discuss building a Europe-Asia Infrastructure Fund.

The most comprehensive plan for investment promotion was proposed in the ASEM Investment Promotion Action Plan (IPAP), called for in the inaugural Asia-Europe Meeting in Bangkok. Thailand convened the ASEM Government and Private Sector Working Group meetings in July 1996 to discuss the drafting of the IPAP, which was later finalized in the second meeting held in Luxembourg in July 1997.

The IPAP proposes an array of activities under two broad pillars: 'Investment Promotion' and 'Investment Policies and Regulations'. As a part of the first pillar, the IPAP proposes building an infrastructure for gathering and servicing information on business and investment issues between the two regions. Furthermore, the IPAP proposes a networking venue for top business leaders under the ASEM Decision-Makers Roundtable, in addition to a working-level exchange programme under ASEM's Business-to-Business Exchange Programme. As a part of the second pillar, the IPAP proposes high-level dialogue among government leaders. European governments and businesses consider developing a transparent and coherent regulatory framework for FDI a high priority under the second pillar. In contrast, many Asian ASEM partners and a relatively high proportion of Asian companies, especially in ASEAN, consider discussions on key regulatory principles such as 'national treatment' irrelevant. However, the majority of Asian companies do deem regulatory principles 'important', since they are also participating in growing degrees of outward FDI.[14]

As it stands, it would be difficult to envision ASEM engaged in negotiations on a multilateral treaty between Asia and European countries in order to develop a regulatory climate for investment liberalization. This is because the current ASEM framework is not a rule-making one. However, ASEM could provide a forum for discussion on developing a regulatory framework for investment liberalization. In addition, ASEM can play the unique role of filtering discussions at the ASEM level before issues move to other international rule-making bodies.

INTERNATIONAL CRUSADE AGAINST BRIBERY AND CORRUPTION

As bribery and corruption are increasingly recognized as barriers to investment and economic growth, the crusade against international bribery has been sweeping across all regions in the world. In Latin America, countries in the OAS (Organization of American States) signed an international convention to combat bribery and to cooperate with member countries on the prosecution of international bribery.[15] On the other side of the Atlantic, there is ongoing work in the European Union on drafting a convention against corruption involving officials of the EU or officials of EU member states. The international movement gained further momentum when the OECD recommended in 1997 that its member economies submit legislation by 1 April 1998, criminalizing bribery of foreign public officials. This legislation would become effective by the end of 1998. In addition to individual legislation, an international convention of OECD member countries is negotiating an agreement to be ratified by the end of 1998 that will criminalize bribery of foreign public officials.

However, this international movement against corruption has not been greeted with enthusiasm everywhere. In particular, Asian countries, leery of the prospects of more intrusive market liberalization by developed countries, opposed bringing up the corruption issue head-on, but included the corruption agenda by agreeing to work on the Multilateral Transparency Agreement to enhance transparency and due process in government procurements.

The resistance by Asian countries can be explained by the fact that Asian countries view the crusade against international corruption as a potential infringement upon their domestic social spheres. Underlying this resistance is Asia's cultural difference from the West in defining what constitutes lawful gift giving and what constitutes illegal bribery, exemplified by Korea's 'rice-cake expenses'.[16] In general, monetary payments to government officials in Korea are not considered bribes, unless the payment results in a reward of some kind. Moreover, to the extent that socially acceptable norms supersede written laws, Asian countries viewed this international movement as the West's attempt to impose its culture on developing countries.

Japan and Korea are unlike other Asian countries in that they are OECD members. Both countries have suffered corruption scandals that have raised the awareness of the importance of fighting corruption. Also, Japan and Korea, as OECD members, will be in a position of criminalizing bribery of foreign public officials by new legislation or amendments to existing ones under peer pressure from regular OECD monitoring. Despite sharing a similar cultural uneasiness that other Asian countries feel towards the fight against corruption, Japan and Korea will be joining other OECD members in the fight against international corruption, once it ratifies the OECD Convention on combating bribery of foreign public officials in international business transactions. Corruption in general should be looked upon as an economic issue that distorts the domestic economy and harms international business. With regard to international corruption, a country's choice boils down to either free riding on a level playing field in investment or contributing to maintaining the level playing field in international business.

The dynamics of the movement against international bribery is such that its momentum is directly proportionate to the total trade and investment of the countries participating in it. In other words, countries participating in the movement have a strong incentive to induce non-participating countries to join the movement. Participating countries have incentive to discourage non-participating countries from free riding on participating countries' self-imposed barriers against giving bribes to foreign officials.

ASEM'S ROLE IN COMBATING CORRUPTION

Asian and European countries alike recognize the importance of promoting a sound environment for FDI flows. The fundamental base for this sound environment lies in guaranteeing national treatment for FDI. The OECD and the WTO are developing a sound regulatory environment for investment liberalization. However, corruption is an investment liberalization issue, which has deeper social dimensions to it. For that reason, the WTO, with the apparent goal of rule making, would probably not be the most appropriate venue to discuss this issue.

A few aspects of ASEM support the possibility that the corruption issue may be dealt with effectively at this level. Firstly, ASEM does not overtly pursue rule making, as does the WTO. Rule making on social issues naturally meets resistance because it is regarded as a threat to sovereignty. In fighting against corruption, it is just as important to 'raise consciousness' as it is to develop multilateral rules. Secondly, ASEM does not have the US as a member. Although the US has led the crusade against international bribery, by excluding the US, the fight against international corruption will shed any image of being a single country's national agenda. Thirdly, ASEM can provide the forums for non-governmental organizations such as the ICC and Transparency International. These organizations have respective regional branches that may lean more towards the position of the parent organization at the international level than the position of the national government. Non-governmental organizations have played a significant role in the fight against corruption, and their efforts can be directly channelled at the ASEM level.

Corruption is the enemy of business. Corruption makes business in foreign countries especially difficult because firms have to take into account the cultural dimension of greasing corrupt bureaucracies and cutting through red tape. Corruption is also no longer a concern for only developed countries. Developing countries need to realize the fact that domestic corruption is detrimental to economic growth. Also, as developing countries grow by exporting, they access foreign markets through subsidiaries by way of FDI. As a result, international corruption hinders developing countries' export promotion efforts.

The fight against corruption should be waged in both domestic as well as international business. However, by distinguishing corruption in international business from that in domestic markets, and by first confronting the former, the international community can avoid pointing fingers at corrupt behaviour in other countries. In this respect, ASEM could provide a balanced forum for first raising consciousness of the adverse effects of corruption in international business and then making concrete proposals to combat them.

REFERENCES

Brittan, Leon,
1995 'Investment Liberalization: the Next Great Boost to the World Economy', *Transnational Corporation* 4, no. 1
Camroux, David and Christian Lechervy
1996 'Close Encounter of a Third Kind? The Inaugural Asia-Europe Meeting of March 1996', *The Pacific Review* 9, no. 3
Kim, Joongi and Jong Bum Kim
1997 'Cultural Differences in the Crusade Against International Bribery: Rice-Cake Expenses in Korea and the Foreign Corrupt Practices Act', *Pacific Rim Law and Policy Journal* 6, no. 3
Mauro, Paolo
1977 'The Effects of Corruption on Growth, Investment, and Government Expenditure: A Cross-Country Analysis', in: Kimberly Ann Elliott, *Corruption and the Global Economy*, Institute for International Economics, Washington DC
Ruggiero, Renato
1996 'Foreign Direct Investment and the Multilateral Trading System', *Transnational Corporations* 5, no. 1
Segal, Gerald
1997 'Thinking Strategically about ASEM: the Subsidiarity Question', *Pacific Review* 10, no. 1

Notes

1. UNCTAD, World Investment Report 1997. The surge in FDI in 1995 partly reflects the cyclical upswing in economic activity for the Group of Seven countries, which are the main suppliers of outward FDI.
2. See Grahm (1995) or Brittan (1995) for more details.
3. *World Economic Outlook*, 1996, fourth quarter.
4. IMF, The Direction of Trade Statistics, *Yearbook*, 1989, 1996.
5. UNCTAD, 'Investing in Asia's Dynamism, European Union Direct Investment in Asia', Joint EU-UNCTAD Study, October, 1996.
6. Id. at 5.
7. Id. at 5.
8. Id. at 5.
9. See Mauro for a review of empirical research on causes and consequences of corruption.

10. OECD document, 'Main Features of the MAI', presented at the symposium on the Multilateral Agreement on Investment, Seoul, Korea, 3-4 April 1997.
11. See Brittan, 1995, for the WTO's future work on developing a multilateral framework for investment liberalization.
12. OECD document, 'Revised Recommendation of the Council on Combating Bribery in International Business Transactions', released May 1997, C(97)123/FINAL.
13. See Shang-Jin Wei, 'How Taxing is Corruption on International Investors' for an empirical analysis of corruption as an investment barrier.
14. See 'The Asia-Europe Investment Promotion Action Plan (IPAP)', 29 July 1997.
15. Inter-American Convention Against Corruption, OAS, 29 March 1996.
16. Discussions of cultural differences in the definition of bribery can be found in Joongi Kim and Jong Bum Kim, 'Cultural Differences in the Crusade Against International Bribery: Rice-Cake Expenses in Korea and the Foreign Corrupt Practices Act', *Pacific Rim Law and Policy Journal* 6, 1997, no. 3.

Developing the Business Relationship between Asia and Europe: Trends and Challenges

Tetsundo Iwakuni

For my presentation, I have been asked to speak on the topic of 'Trends and Challenges in the Business Relationship for Asia in Europe'. Having spent thirty years in the financial industry in Japan, Europe, and the United States before entering the world of politics, I cannot help but take an approach to this topic based on my past and present experience. Because my area of expertise lies in Japan rather than Asia, I have tried, throughout this article, to use the Japanese case to draw out generalizations and to comment on ways in which they may either apply or not apply to Asia as a whole.

In addressing this topic, it is important to keep in mind the difficulty of generalizing on trends and challenges for Asian countries, since it would be problematic to characterize any one pattern as being 'typical' for all of Asia. Whereas we can increasingly talk of Europe as one bloc with the further integration and realization of the European Union, Asia incorporates Japan, (which has had its own singular model of development), the ASEAN countries, and other high-potential economic powers such as China, that cannot fall into a common category with other Asian countries.

However, if we were to let this difficulty deter us from any further examination, this would be the end of my article. So, let us say that we *can* identify some common trends and challenges for Asia in the last decade or two. What would these be?

I have organized some of the observable trends into three categories: overall trends, trade-related trends, and capital market trends. Many of the challenges that face Asia are, for obvious reasons, associated with the aforementioned trends, and therefore will be discussed conjointly. Nonetheless, there are challenges in three basic areas - environment, political culture and social ethics, and education - that I feel are significant enough to warrant special attention.

As described above, it is difficult to generalize for all of Asia. There is no *one* typical Asian country and patterns are not necessarily applicable to every single economy in Asia. However, if we can indeed identify some common trends in the last decade or two, the following cannot be ignored.

Overall Trends

First are those overall trends that affect the whole world, including Asia. One such direction is 'globalization'. We are witnessing increased trends toward international mergers and acquisitions, overseas direct investment, tax systems and overseas production. Transnational companies are setting up their head offices on two or more continents; more and more companies are 'bicultural', e.g. Rhone-Poulenc Rorer (France and USA), and other pharmaceutical companies.

Another trend often associated with globalization is 'localization,' involving increased emphasis on hiring host country nationals to staff and manage overseas operations.

Third, there is a generalized desire to maintain an economic balance of power. This includes efforts to prevent any one country or economy, notably the United States, from a super-dominant position at the global scale. At regional levels, this trend is reflected in the feeling that Germany should not dominate the EU, or in concerns that only Japan or China might dominate the Asian economy.

As far as Asia is concerned, many economies have, for the last decade or so, been enjoying high growth rates, and relatively low labour costs.

Trade-Related Trends

Asian economies have long been characterized for their pattern of export-oriented economic expansion. However, a more recent trend is towards reverse imports, in other words producing overseas and re-importing back to Asia (e.g. American-made Hondas, European-made electronic products). This is of course a natural result of the above-mentioned two currents: globalization and localization. Overseas production allows manufacturers to globalize their product design, be close to the market, and localize both sourcing of materials and sales.

Second, the tendency to reap the greatest profits at the lowest cost, which is the spirit of international competition, will become even more fierce in the future.

Third, Asian companies, as we are well aware, have been known to excel in mass production and mass marketing for a mass consumption market. However, a more advanced and sophisticated market in Europe means that the European consumer, instead of wanting to be exactly like his neighbour, wants to distinguish, or differentiate, himself from others. Whereas Asian consumers have traditionally sought to acquire 'standard' products, and, at least in the case of Japan, there was much pressure to obtain what the 'other people' have, the situation is quite different in Europe. Therefore, the new trend, which can also be considered a challenge, is to what extent Asian companies will be successful in a move away from 'mass production of few product lines', to 'smaller quantity production of diverse goods and services for a more discerning consumer market'.

CAPITAL MARKET TRENDS

So far, I have discussed trends in the trade relationship between Asia and Europe, but I now turn to a discussion of the financial and capital markets.

Asia has a very close trading relationship with the United States. In the world of money and capital markets, on the other hand, Asia, and especially Japan, has long enjoyed a much closer relationship with Europe. As we all know, the supply and demand of capital varies greatly from country to country within Europe, just as in Asia. However, in contrast to Asia, European market mechanisms are more sophisticated and function more efficiently. As a result, Asian countries turned to European capital markets not only for the redistribution of Asian capital, but also as a means to raise capital from Europe. In other words, Europe's surplus capital has in effect supported Asian growth and Asian infrastructure.

All this ironically came about because of Kennedy's Interest Equalization Tax, which took effect in July 1963. This IET meant that non-US borrowers were taxed one per cent whenever they tapped the US capital markets. Thus, the US effectively rejected and shut out European and Asian governments and private industries by penalizing such foreign entities. This was known as the 'Kennedy shock' and caused the Japanese stock market to plummet. Asian countries were forced to seek relatively cheaper capital elsewhere, resulting in the convergence on the European capital markets. Although this financial 'wall', the IET, was repealed in 1989, Japan, during the period 1963-1996, ended up raising 70 times more in European capital markets than in the United States.

One could say that Kennedy's 'big ban', in 1963 led to the 'big bang' of 1986. However, the status quo - with the US-Japan relationship focused on trade and the Japan-Europe relationship focused on money - is not acceptable. In the future, Asia's trade and financial relationships must become more global in nature because trade markets and money markets go hand in hand. Therefore, it is important to expand the trade relationship between Asia and Europe in the future. In this sense, this 'trend' also represents a new 'challenge' for Asia in Europe.

ENVIRONMENT

Most of the so-called 'developed' countries are becoming more environmentally conscious. Consumers in some of the Western European countries have been known to base their purchasing decisions on political or humanitarian ethics, as when stockholders divested themselves of shares in companies doing business with apartheid South Africa. We see also a trend in the US and Europe to make consumer decisions partly based on whether or not a company is environmentally friendly. Asian companies will find that 'green' products are not at a disadvantage when marketing in Europe.

The heightened awareness of the interdependence between man and nature, of the global warming effects that are not limited to just one region of the world, means that the whole 'environment' in which companies produced, marketed, and sold, has changed radically. No longer is it acceptable, as it was thirty, even twenty years ago, for any one country to aggressively pursue industrialization at the expense of environmental safety.

Should a particular industry or a particular country ignore such warnings, there is a risk that there may be 'punitive actions' taken. Such counter measures could come from international organizations, individual governments, or, spontaneously, at the level of the individual end user. Asian companies, used to operating more often than not in a more lax context, will increasingly be faced with the need to address this issue if they are to be successful in their business relationships with Europe.

On the other hand, of course, the argument, and it is not one without cause, is that for decades, the more developed nations and industries which continued to enjoy growth with disregard for this issue, did so before the environment became a social and political issue. This argument claims furthermore that to impose restrictions on production processes out of environmental concern is tantamount to a protectionist measure taken by the already developed nations.

The more developed economies could ignore this argument while maintaining a hard line, by placing all responsibility for operating within certain environmental standards on the developing economies and industries. However, our environment knows no frontiers. In this sense both Asia and Europe share a common destiny. Precisely because this issue is of mutual concern, there should be serious cooperation on a global level to share the kind of technology and knowledge that will allow the developing nations to continue industrialization without undue damage to the environment, so that we may all benefit.

Today, there is no such thing as prosperity at the expense of others. Pursuit of pure economic profit will inevitably take second place in our priorities if this earth is no longer able to sustain its population. The measure of success should not be limited to the one area of the economy, such as the level of GNP. Rather, as we enter the next century, we should all challenge ourselves to consider the true wealth of a nation in terms of GHP, or Gross Happiness and Prosperity. To transform this mentality will be a true challenge, not only for Asia, but for the whole world.

POLITICAL CULTURE AND SOCIAL ETHICS

Japan's financial sector is finally at the dawn of an era of true competition because Japan's version of the 'big bang' will radically liberalize its banking and securities industries. As one of the first steps, in April 1998, Japan's foreign exchange markets will be completely liberalized. As a result, 10 trillion dollars in domestic Japanese personal savings will be able to flow more freely across national borders and into international markets. Later, regulations that have prevented banks, insurance companies, and securities firms from competing with each other for many decades will be removed.

It is sad, however, to learn as final versions of the plans for Japan's Big Bang were being drawn up, that two of Japan's most high-ranking financial firms had been involved in some of the most shocking scandals ever seen.

Over a period of thirty years, roughly 50 employees of Nomura Securities, including its former chairman and vice chairman, spent time training at Merrill Lynch in the US and returned to key positions in Nomura's new product development division and the international division. In New York, those trainees learned everything they could about the art and strategy of making money. Judging from the recent scandals, however, one thing they did not spend enough time learning about is that upholding the law is the basis of doing business in the United States. It seems that as long as it is good for the company, illegal and unethical activities are acceptable in Japan, even illicit transactions with organized crime, paying off racketeers and guaranteeing profits for VIPs. These kinds of illicit activities are not tolerated in the financial centres of North America and Europe.

This kind of corruption could only have arisen out of an atmosphere where close connections with powerful politicians and Ministry of Finance officials enabled one to get away with virtually anything. The Ministry of Finance used an elaborate web of regulations to carefully divide Japan's financial market into many small territories so that competition actually could not occur. Because profits were almost guaranteed by this system, people did not use their heads to think of creative new financial products as much as they used their heads to bow to the politicians and bureaucrats.

This kind of relationship is popularly referred to as the 'iron triangle', but perhaps the term 'crooked triangle' would be more appropriate. At the time corruption became common in the manufacturing and finance industries, the bigger you were, the stronger. In Japan, if you were strong enough, then you could even avoid prosecution in the courts for your illegal activities.

If there is anything to be learned from Japan's case, and specifically its mistakes, it is that Japan's relationship with Europe cannot change unless Japan's domestic economic and political structures also change. If Japan is able to reform its domestic economic and political structures, then a stronger relationship with Europe and more business opportunities are sure to follow.

Under the leadership of Prime Minister Margaret Thatcher, England carried out difficult reforms that brought its financial markets in line with international financial market standards. As a result, both England and the world economy have prospered. Japan must learn from England's 'big bang' experience. If Japan's financial markets cannot only be made more efficient but also more open to international capital flows and foreign financial institutions, then the potential business gains for Europe would be enormous. The Japanese political system is based on European political systems. Because of the similarity of the systems, there is much that Japan can learn from the European experience in promoting open and discrimination-free political systems. This issue is critical because successful reform of the Japanese political system is just as important for the Japanese as it will be for the peoples of Europe.

For this reason, one cannot overlook the importance of education in promoting the kind of crucial and fundamental understanding among the peoples of both continents. The essential question is this: *What* will Asia be learning from Europe, and *how* will it adapt that knowledge back home?

EDUCATION

So far, I have noted the need for a country like Japan to learn from Europe's political systems and economic structures. However, learning from Europe should go much beyond these 'hard' elements, and encompass those more nebulous areas of 'culture' and 'human understanding'. As is evident in the example of Nomura that I shared above, a simple exchange of technical knowledge about business practices and strategies is not sufficient to ensure the development of a certain kind of attitude and awareness that will be necessary to encourage the growth of healthy business relationships between Asia and Europe built on respect.

PROMOTING MORE EDUCATION EXCHANGE OPPORTUNITIES BETWEEN ASIA AND EUROPE

According to UNESCO's 1996 *Statistical Yearbook*, during the last ten years, the overall number of Japanese students studying abroad has increased by approximately 300 per cent. The number of these students headed for the US showed an increase of approximately 300 per cent, while those going to the UK increased by 500 per cent. On the other hand, Japanese students studying in France increased by only 30 per cent, and those going to Germany, 5 per cent. While these figures are only relative, and are not representative of Asia, what they do indicate to us is that there is a two-tier 'market' of foreign student destinations: English-speaking and non English-speaking countries. Moreover, in terms of absolute enrolment numbers, the United States hosts the largest number of international students, more than the next three leading nations - France, Germany, and the UK combined.

Let us now look at how Asia is represented in these countries.[1] In 1992, while approximately 15 per cent of national foreign enrolment in France was from Asia, this figure was approximately 42 per cent for Germany, and 40 per cent in the UK. Asian students in the United States, on the other hand, represented over 65 per cent of total foreign enrolment. This figure was over 90 per cent for Japan. Although there is the obvious argument of geographic proximity, these figures clearly paint the enormous challenge faced by both Asia and Europe in the field of international education exchange.

This situation represents a serious challenge, especially for those non English-speaking European countries, because international educational exchange is essential in ensuring mutual understanding of languages, cultures, economies, and societies. Without this constant two-way flow of real information and personal contact, relations between Asia and Europe, whether business or otherwise, can only become stagnant at best, and antagonistic at worst. In this sense, the responsibility for an initiative in this area falls on both Asian and European private and public sectors.[2]

Thus, for increased exposure of our youth to meaningful cross-cultural experiences, we need to promote more university exchange programmes between Asia and Europe. As with the EU's highly successful ERASMUS programme, such initiatives should not be left entirely to individual academic institutions, but should benefit from public sector encouragement and political leadership.

Improving the Quality of International Exchange

Increasing the number of international educational exchange programmes is certainly important. However, we need also to ensure that the contents of all such international experiences, whether academic or work-related, are rich enough to encourage real learning. As the Nomura case illustrates, professional development should not be limited to technical skills and knowledge, but should extend to learning about those fundamental 'premises' and 'givens' of a particular country (i.e. about those invisible rules that dictate human action that we call 'culture').

In recent years, there has been an explosive increase in the numbers of Japanese students pursuing their studies overseas, as well as a noticeable increase in the numbers of foreign students studying in Japan. According to UNESCO figures for 1994 (as quoted in the 1996 *Statistical Yearbook*), there were an overwhelming 43,770 Japanese students in the United States. In comparison, there were only 1,157 Japanese students in France, 1,236 in Germany, and 2,042 in England. Looking at the number of foreign students studying in Japan shows a very different situation.

According to Japanese Ministry of Education's figures for 1996, most of Japan's foreign student population (52,921 - or over 90 per cent) comes from other Asian countries. In contrast, only 1,088 students from the US and only several hundred from Europe are studying in Japan.

In order to improve this situation, the Japanese Ministry of Education set out to more than double the number of foreign students studying in Japan from just over 40,000 to 100,000 by the year 2000. Regrettably, by 1996 the number had reached a plateau of approximately 56,000, far short of the goal.

The Japanese government's emphasis on numbers alone, however, portrays a somewhat shallow or superficial understanding of the value of educational exchange. As noted earlier, a mere exchange of knowledge is not enough. It is not by having larger numbers of foreign students pass through Japan that we can congratulate ourselves on the quality of their learning experience; this rule applies equally to all host countries. Unfortunately, students participating in educational exchange programmes, and even foreign expatriates, can often be seen socializing mostly amongst themselves - perhaps due to homesickness or frustration from not being able to communicate in a foreign language. The reasons notwithstanding, the result is that these international visitors do not necessarily gain more than a marginal understanding of the culture and way of thinking while studying or working overseas.

EMPHASIZING INTERCULTURAL EDUCATION

International exchange programmes commonly cite that one of the main objectives is to promote mutual understanding. If we are truly committed to this goal, then we must put much more serious thought into developing the kinds of educational exchange programmes that will provide the participants not only with a fulfilling academic experience, but also with a more profound appreciation and understanding of the differences in culture and alternative viewpoints.

Intercultural experts have become aware of these fundamental cultural differences between peoples - differences that for example, influence one's value judgements, one's moral or ethical judgements of good and bad, right and wrong. What appears 'natural' in one culture is not necessarily 'natural' in another, and these kinds of basic differences can evolve into misunderstandings, and can even be magnified into outright conflicts.

In the area of professional training and internships, ignorance of such 'soft' knowledge and cross-cultural understanding can directly affect bottom-line business performance.

The Samsung Group, a Korean conglomerate, realized that there was an urgent need to completely rethink the structure and content of employee education. It decided to take bold measures not only in terms of manufacturing or operations, but also in the area of 'globalizing' its employees if it was to continue to expand dynamically well into the 21st century. As far as I know, it is the one major Asian company that has instituted such an ambitious programme to enable its employees to take one full year overseas, at regular pay, in whatever country they choose, doing whatever they desire. Many select to spend time studying in Europe, and return to Samsung as 'regional experts'. In addition, it has established an institute dedicated to equipping future expatriates with 'hard' skills related to globalization, as well as to such 'soft' skills as cross-cultural understanding and communication.

It is true that an Asian company launched this initiative. However, as long as the move toward a global economy continues, and we cannot yet foresee the reversal of such a trend, European businesses will also profit from rising to the challenge of nurturing intercultural sensitivity in their key personnel. Samsung thus serves as a model for other Asian and European private sector initiatives.

Therefore, for all the reasons raised above, I believe European public and private sectors should do more to encourage initiatives in international exchange, and to ensure its depth and quality. It is a matter of mutual benefit, mutual responsibility, and mutual challenge for both Asia and Europe.

Conclusion

In summary, when we consider business relations between Asia and Europe, we often tend to think only of trade relations, as exemplified by how the Asian press expressed, in the past, concern about the European Fortress, that is, the EU and its potentially prohibitive barriers to Asian imports. It is true that in order to comply with certain EU specifications, it was necessary for more companies from Asian countries, such as the Korean conglomerates or Japanese multinationals, to make massive investments within the EU.

At the same time, however, one must acknowledge the great opportunity the EU represents for Asia. Europe, just like Asia, is diverse not only in terms of the numerous cultures and languages, but also in terms of the multiple goods and services, telecommunication, and electrical standards (e.g. different electrical plugs, video or TV systems). But with the growing standardization of specifications within the EU, Asian countries will be able to market a uniform product that will be compatible in all those countries.

In addition, because European countries constitute a wide variety of peoples with varying languages and cultures living in close quarters, they have been involved in a difficult process of developing international norms and setting common standards. This process of international integration has helped the peoples of Europe to both secure the benefits of international trade as well as to decrease the likelihood of friction. Asian countries also constitute a collection of diverse peoples, and could learn a great deal from the European experience in order to address some of the similar challenges.

Ultimately, the challenges outlined above can also be considered opportunities for Asia in Europe. I feel that this attitude or perspective of seeing challenges as opportunities rather than obstacles will greatly influence the degree to which both Asia and Europe shall be willing to persevere in their efforts to overcome barriers and frustrations and the degree of commitment each will have in developing mutual understanding.

In conclusion, I hope that one of the themes that has emerged from this article is that the most important business trends and challenges for Asia in Europe cannot necessarily be found in any particular business ventures, investment opportunities or new technology. There is now widespread accessibility to and adaptation of industrial knowledge and technology, and greater Asian foreign direct investment in Europe is expected to continue.

Rather, the underlying business challenge for Asia in Europe lies in an area that many Asian businessmen and government officials - Japanese ones in particular - have mostly overlooked: culture, political and social ethics, and business practices. It seems that many have often assumed that there is just one economic language, their own, only one way to do business, their own, and that misunderstandings or complications in bilateral relationships were simply inconveniences or obstacles that could not be avoided.

However, with growing awareness that such 'obstacles' arise from differences in culture, ethics, or language, we can now address the need to encourage intercultural experiences that are truly significant for both students and professionals in business. These initiatives, on either continent, should operate at all levels of society, whether from international organizations, the businesses, private individuals, or in the form of official government programmes. After all, mutual understanding is not only rewarding for both Asia and Europe, but is essential for our survival.

Finally, I believe that mutual prosperity is guaranteed for Europe and Asia as long as we continue efforts toward mutual understanding through the next century. Nevertheless, what I can also affirm is that mutual prosperity will never come if Europe or Asia ever discontinues that effort. Indeed, this is the real threat, the real challenge imposed on ourselves; thus, it is not from without, not from any one superpower domination, and not from any specific economic bloc.

Notes

1. Todd M. Davis (ed.) *Open Doors, Report on International Educational Exchange, 1994/95*, Institute of International Education, pp. 81-2.
2. In addition, from the European point of view, we can consider this issue as one of *economic impact*, i.e. the *export value of international students*. A country is considered to 'export' educational services if foreign students study at its academic institutions. According to a study by David Greenaway and Jacqueline Tuck at the University of Nottingham (*Economic Impact of International Students in UK Higher Education*), for example, this 'export value' of students fully funded by overseas sources amounted to as much as £716 million for 1992-3 (calculated as the sum of education fees of £310 million and £406 million in other expenditures on UK produces goods and services). This figure represents over twice the value of UK exports of coal, gas, and electricity in the same year. Therefore, it is also in Europe's economic interest to encourage such international student exchanges.

The Future of ASEM

Assessing China's Impact on Asia-EU Relations

Zhao Gancheng

Concerning China's impact on Asia-EU relations, the first question one might raise is what impact China would have on Asia precisely because China is going to be an Asian power with certain global influence. Therefore, on the one hand, in developing Asia-EU relations, China will be one of the members of the Asian family, though it will have its own interests to pursue. China will not represent Asia in dealing with the EU, nor will China lead Asia. On the other hand, since China is already a big power in Asia, its relations with the EU, especially with the major countries of the EU, will become a significant part of the whole of Asia-EU relations. Starting from this perspective, this paper will analyse three issues.

The Trend of China's Domestic Development and External Behaviour

Since China launched the reform programme in 1979, the nation has been sustaining relatively rapid economic growth, leading to a significant increase of its national power. With fast development not necessarily only confined to economic growth, it has also faced a variety of new issues that were not conceivable under the old planned economy such as: how to revitalize the large quantity of state-owned enterprises which are losing money in the new market-driven operating system; how to resettle millions of laid-off workers from the non-effective state-owned enterprises, who could not possibly appreciate any leadership, whether democratic or authoritative, if there are no jobs available to them; how to make the state interference more effective in terms of reducing the income disparity which is unfortunately yet increasing to an even larger extent; and how to protect the environment while continuing the industrialization process, especially in interior China, a large part of which is still in extreme poverty, etc. In other words, lots of people suddenly find that the quicker the development pace, the more problems the nation would have. But the Chinese leadership, whether during the Deng Xiaoping era, or after his death, always insists that continuing the reform will be the one and only solution to these problems. It is like being on a bike that cannot stop, lest it fall down. Insofar as the current situation is concerned, people tend to agree that there is no demarcation line between the Deng Xiaoping era and post-Deng era, at least in economic terms. This has significant implications relating to the trend of China's development in the next decade.

Firstly, in the economic area, since China's economic reform cannot be separated from its opening policy and since its future economic growth would, in a large part, depend on its external economic exchanges, it would have to make more efforts to integrate itself into the world economic system, by, among other things, continuing to work hard for the entry into the WTO and to enhance its economic and trading relations with other countries, especially with the developed nations and the Asian Newly Industrialized Economies (NIEs). This is simply because China will have no other way to go along. There are some other arguments which suggest that China pursue its interests by strengthening exchanges, including economic ones, with the developing countries, particularly when political stability between China and the developed nations is being threatened, and China must be ready to face a serious setback of its relations with, say, the United States and even Japan. But the fact that the economic integrity in global economic development is indivisible would hardly prove the effectiveness of this approach for China.

The economic lessons China has had over the last decade do not teach that its economic links with the developed nations are decreasing in importance. Politically, it might be the right thing for China to shift its attention to the developing countries, but it would give far less support to China's domestic economic enhancement, which is the most important target for the nation in the next decade, and which is, according to the Chinese leadership, also the reliable solution to the problems surfacing in its society. So, the point is that China might not be able to afford to cut off its economic links with the West if it wants to consolidate its reform results already achieved and to further liberalize its economic operating system for a finally complete integration into the world system. On China's part, such links not only mean advanced technology and foreign capital, which are, of course, very important to China, but also further interdependence between China and the developed countries, which is so far the best guarantee for preventing minor friction from turning into a total deterioration as proven by the latest debate on the extension of China's MFN status in the US last Spring. Secondly, while China has to enhance its economic links with the West in order to promote domestic development, it does not mean that the increasing dependence of China would reduce its self-confidence to the extent that it would have to accept whatsoever the West wishfully imposes on it. This is particularly important in the political sense.

As indicated by all the public statements and official policies of China, the post-Deng Chinese leadership would continue to give first priority to economic reform and the building-up of what is known as 'the socialist market economy', which will, in turn, require political stability. This political stability, domestically, means the least possible interruption of gradual social development and gradual political progress including more political transparency and participation. This means, externally, resistance of pressure from the outside, especially from the West, which focuses on value distinction, and from the Chinese perspective, is ill-intended. This is then a very controversial issue in the West, which might well trace back to the protracted Rites Controversy of the 17th and early 18th centuries when the Jesuits, in taking Christianity to China, insisted upon the universality and exclusivity of their religion: to be religious, the Chinese would have had to abandon their own cultural sensibilities. But the failure of the Rome establishment in its China mission, to which less Chinese than expected had committed,[1] seems not to have given a good lesson. On the contrary, the mentality of universality has taken its modern form as prevailing political human rights. As Mr Ames suggests, if freedom is good wine, America has become an alcoholic.[2] Probably most Western countries are also alcoholics when they handle this issue with other nations that have their own distinctive tradition, culture and history. This is precisely one of the main debates between China and the West.

In principle, China does not deny the righteousness of freedom as well as other political human rights. But just as it is not right to advise an adolescent to take strong alcohol, China is deeply suspicious of the Western purpose to impose so much pressure on China, the target of which might well be to set obstacles to China's normal growth, and to destroy China's political stability. The latest example is China's serious protest by the Foreign Affairs Committee of the National People's Congress on 13 June 1997, against the European Parliament Resolution on the Communication from the European Commission on a long-term Policy for China-Europe Relations, which was issued on 12 June 1997. Though the resolution is not binding for concerned decision makers, it attacks China on a number of issues including human rights. The Chinese People's Congress immediately called it 'Anti-China clamour',[3] because it believed the resolution tried to change China's values and system by imposing pressure, which according to the Chinese statement, is a totally wrong calculation. So, in the foreseeable future, China's political will to keep stability in order to promote economic development will be in conflict with the fact that few Western countries genuinely appreciate China's reality and efforts.

Thirdly, in military and security areas, China's domestic development over the decade indicates an inclination towards defence modernization, which has expectedly caused controversies in the international community. There is little doubt that China is making great efforts to modernize its military, although its defence expenditure in absolute terms is yet far less than that of all the other big powers, even less than that of some middle powers. Most Chinese military experts argue that the nation's current military status has long been too poor to defend its mainland, let alone its marine territory.[4] China is making greater efforts in the post-Cold War era only because its rapid economic growth and corresponding increase of its national power have made it possible. It has much more to do with China's own need for a sufficient self-defence rather than to the forthcoming reconfiguration of the world system at the end of the Cold War. From a Chinese perspective, the national priority should be given to economic development, though, its efforts in defence modernization must continue. But the fact that China is already a big power in Asia might cause suspicion among other Asian nations of China's accelerating pace of defence modernization.

The issue is then what kind of purpose it will serve. Will China be more aggressive when it is more powerful? There are already many hypotheses, although it would be meaningless to seek a definite answer. Ordinary Chinese would like to look to history, to try and find some trace. Chinese history hardly gives any convincing examples to illustrate an aggressive China even when the nation was the most powerful in the world. On the contrary, when the power centre shifted to the West and the civilized West turned towards Asia with their aggressive pirate spirit, submissive as China always was, the nation could never have been able to turn around its 'loser' status, only suffering too much from being humiliated. Most Chinese, whether leadership, academics, or ordinary people, believe it was only due to the fact that the nation was too weak. They might feel hardly convinced that a militarily weak China would possibly be in the nation's interest. This kind of sentiment has underlined the increasing efforts in defence modernization, which, in the Chinese view, is totally justified as long as the nation continues to pursue a peaceful and independent foreign policy.

Another argument for justifying defence modernization is that, in history, China has never been an expansionist country. It is not because China was too weak to expand, but because the Chinese traditions, culture and morals were such that aggressive behaviour in dealing with other countries was not appreciated. What China wants is dignity, respect, independence and legitimate interests, which China did not get in the past because it was too weak both politically and militarily. China will not expand even when it is powerful. Instead, a more powerful China will become a strong stabilizer in maintaining peace in the region precisely because most of the chaos taking place in Asia in modern history was related to a weak China. Whether one trusts the Chinese official statement that 'we will never seek for hegemony',[5] China's determination that military modernization must be one of its national targets in the coming years will not change.

These domestic trends will have significant impact on China's external behaviour. On the one hand, China's priority given to the reform programme and sustained economic growth will require a more open China and increasingly close relations with the outside world, especially with the developed nations, of which, the EU is one of the three pillars. China must actively integrate itself into the global economy and participate in the ever-increasing economic exchanges. In doing so, China must observe all the universally accepted norms and practically reform its old regulations and systems that are not part of the international practices. China will have to further its efforts to join the WTO in order to become a genuine part of the world economic system. Necessary concessions that will make China's entry more accepted may be made provided they would not do much harm to its national interests. In other words, the process that started one and half decades ago to open the nation to the outside world is likely to continue in the post-Deng era, and China will try its best to strengthen its economic links with the West.

But this is unlikely to be done at the expense of China's pursuit of domestic political stability, nor will China give up its military modernization process. Faced with the controversies, China will try every means to win the trust of other nations, especially its Asian neighbours, no matter how difficult it would be. Issues like implementing the 'one country, two systems' after the Hong Kong hand-over and the territory disputes over the South China Sea islands between China and some Southeast Asian nations will show China's intention of confidence-building measures, and the image China will give to the world. More importantly, China's pursuit of a peaceful and independent foreign policy determines that it would more likely adopt a moderate attitude towards regional affairs because what China hopes to achieve in the coming years is to maintain stability in its periphery so that the nation could concentrate itself on domestic problems. But this should not lead to an incorrect conclusion that China would pursue a stable periphery at the expense of its fundamental national interests such as indivisible sovereignty and national integrity, which will be extremely sensitive for China in the coming years.

On the other hand, while economic relations between China and the West are expected to increase, political ones will depend on many variables. One of them might be how the West sees China's role in Asia, the other being the extent to which China is determined to resist pressure from the West. Both of them would trigger off emotional behaviours easily. If the West, and even worse, if other Asian nations, especially the Southeast Asian nations, see China as a potential threat or a future hegemony in Asia, domestic debates on their respective China policy could be more tense as proven by the debates in the US over recent years. That would create a more difficult environment for China to build up peaceful and stable relations with other countries. The fact that the

West, led by the US, will continue to impose pressure on China in a number of areas including the human rights issues, trade issues, and particularly the ideological issues involving China's political system, is a complication which has time and again led to China's radical reactions. Some scholars argue that it is the consequence of the Chinese leadership's efforts to strengthen nationalist sentiments labelled as 'conservative'.[6] But in terms of cause and effect, even if this nationalism is being strengthened, the Western pressure on China, which has been increasing since the end of the Cold War, must be the major trigger. The popularity of books like *China Can Say 'No'*[7] in the 1990s is not accidental. As a matter of fact, China will not give up its efforts to enhance its relations with other powers, but such interaction between China and the West will likely continue, which implies a dangerous trend.

CHINA'S POSITION IN ASIA AND ITS IMPACT ON ASIA-EU RELATIONS

As an Asian power with some global influence, China's position in the region has been increasingly important over the decades, as the nation has been focusing on domestic development. It is interesting to note that, during the 1960s when the nation took on the track of a revolutionary ideology with an outward-oriented strategy, its influence in the region was far less than now, where it concentrates more on its domestic affairs. This is certainly due to the increase of its national power, which has resulted from the sustained rapid economic growth and opening policy.

When the Cold War was over, China faced very serious questions. One of them was whether China would follow the former Soviet Union. At this turning point, while the West might have been happily waiting for what would be, in their view, the inevitable, it was more possible for China's Asian neighbours to watch nervously. In retrospect, China could have had three alternatives: first, continuing the reform programme with the risk of political transformation that might have thrown China into chaos, but maintaining political stability would not be entirely impossible; second, turning inward and resisting all kinds of pressure to keep order, which would have killed the reform programme that had achieved so much over the 1980s, but the immediate danger would have been much less; and third, starting political transformation as soon as possible to release the pressure but with the eminent danger of disintegration as the former Soviet Union had already experienced.

With his political wisdom as a great statesman, Deng Xiaoping chose the first alternative. Beginning with the early 1990s, China has been intensifying its efforts to restructure its economic system and accelerate the pace of economic marketization. In the meantime, political reform has also been well under way but in a gradual and controlled manner, demonstrated by an increase of political transparency and reinforcement of the legal system. The wisdom of this strategy has been well recognized throughout the world, leading to substantial improvement of the nation's economic power and living standards, and to a great promotion of China's position in Asia.

Coincidentally, China's domestic development has been taking place while the reconfiguration of the international system in the Asia-Pacific has been under way. The collapse of the bipolar system requires a replacement, which could, of course, have a variety of possibilities. But with the increase of the weight of other powers, one thing may be for sure: that the American dominance in the region would become less likely if a new structure of balance of power would emerge, in which the China-factor might become decisive. There are two reasons for that. One is that the size, population and geopolitical position of China in Asia determines that a stable international system in the Asia-Pacific would not be feasible without China's active participation. The other is that China's intensifying efforts to integrate itself into the world community and its successful economic growth make it more possible than ever for China to play a positive role as a stabilizer. The initiative for the Asia-Europe Meeting by the ASEAN and the EU decided to include China, Japan and Korea as participants. This meeting reflects the reality of the power structure in Asia.

That China is becoming a decisive factor in the formation of the new balance of power in the Asia-Pacific region has important implications in terms of China's rapport with the EU and its impact on Asia-EU relations.

1. Since Asia is the fastest developing region in the world and China is its largest part, the EU may take increasing interest in developing relations with Asia not only focusing on economic benefits but on political and cultural exchanges as well. If China's weight in Asia increases, presumably, the EU would pay more attention to it in the sense that the EU would consider it part of the Asian community rather than an alien or unique entity. While the new international order in the Asia-Pacific will yet be made through the efforts of the nation-states in the region that are diversified, China, though not dominant at all, will play an indispensable role in the Asian family. If the EU wants to build up a stable and mutual beneficiary relationship with Asia, it would have to pay increasing attention to its relations with China corresponding to the increase of China's national power and its position in the region.

2. In economic terms, China's enormous potential has been well recognized, and the Chinese market has become a great backup for sustained growth in the whole region. China's contribution to the rapid growth of the Asian economy has helped to establish a fair and rational economic order, which, by nature, should not go against the interests of the West, but which would not accept the Western dominance in the long-term either. It is for this purpose that Asia must

have an equal dialogue with the West, particularly with the Unites States and the EU. In addition to the APEC, the first Asia-Europe Meeting was generally regarded as a demonstration of and a good start for the dialogue. The historic meaning of the meeting reflects the common desire of both the ASEAN and the EU to play a more positive role in the post-Cold War era. Doubtless, the participation of China as well as the other Asian nations upgraded the importance of the meeting.

Such dialogue is a continuing process, during which the Asian position in the global economy is increasingly important, but it would be inconceivable that Asia could have an effective dialogue with the West without China's active participation. For if Asia wants to have more say in this process, its voice must include that of China. By the same token, as the EU's involvement in Asia grows broader in scope, its Asia policy can not possibly be complete without significant guidelines for China. In fact, as Sir Leon Brittan, Vice President of the European Commission, commented on the Hong Kong hand-over, '(EU) relations with Hong Kong as its history enters a new phase (the hand-over) fit well into Europe's overall Asia strategy',[8] which certainly implies the significance of China from the EU perspective. Of course, the Hong Kong Special Administrative Region has its unique status and obligations, but the prosperity of this area, the great vitality of its economy, and the opening of the city are nevertheless the symbol of modern China. The fact that Hong Kong now is part of China's sovereignty and the increasing economic interdependence between mainland China and Hong Kong also point to the accelerating pace of China's integration into the international community.

3. China's desire to sustain rapid economic growth and to play a proper role in maintaining peace and stability in the region requires the nation to promote relations with its neighbours and the Western powers. The Chinese official policy seems to be dominated by such guidelines for maintaining the stability of its periphery by pursuing peaceful and friendly relations with all the Asian neighbours and by objecting to the use of force to solve disputes and problems remaining from the Cold War. This peaceful foreign policy is based on the awareness of increasing interdependence and enormous benefits that have been reaped by China due to the stable periphery. This stability serves a domestic purpose, that is, to enable the nation to concentrate on economic development and surging domestic problems. If China does not change its priority, (personally, I don't think there is any substantial reason why China should change), it might be safe to predict that China will continue to pursue this policy, though unstable factors do exist.[9]

4. That China would continue to pursue a peaceful foreign policy should have significant implications for Asia-EU relations. A stable and prosperous Asia is the basis of healthy Asia-EU relations and stability and prosperity of Asia are closely related to China's domestic development and external be-

haviour. If China was chaotic or aggressive, Asia would suffer; and if Asia was in turmoil, enormous interests of the West including that of the EU would be at stake.

5. In addition to its efforts to be on good terms with its Asian neighbours, China will try every means to develop good relations with the West, on the basis of non-interference of each other's internal affairs (an important principle that China is likely to adhere to in the coming years). In this pursuit, the EU accounts for a very, if not the most, important part because China is clearly aware of the stakes. During the Cold War, only as a political power, China considered the EU as a counterweight against the Soviets out of China's own geo-strategic thinking. This factor has now gone, but as the most developed area in the world, the EU has become one of the sources for China's economic take-off in terms of technology, capital, management and so on. Recent years have seen a large increase of economic exchanges between China and the major EU countries, France and Germany in particular. China believes such promotion is conducive not only to economic interests of concerned parties, but also to better mutual understanding and communication, including political dialogue. There is little doubt that China would like to collaborate with the EU, just as it has already built up a strategic partnership with Russia, if it wants to play a proper role in the emerging new structure in the Asia-Pacific.

6. Suppose China's domestic development continues without major interruption, that is, that China would be able to maintain an average annual GDP growth rate at 7 per cent to 8 per cent in the next decade.[10] What will it do to Asia-EU relations? This is really a challenging question. Although by the year 2010, according to China's official estimate, the GNP per capita of the nation would be around USD 1,500; its economic size and its totality would produce a great market the world may have never seen. As one member of the Asian family, China's contribution to the region would be indispensable in a variety of areas in terms of building up a more solid relationship between Asia and the EU. As the EU's involvement in Asia is expected to deepen, interdependence between China and the major European countries may rise to such an extent that neither side could afford a breakdown over minor interruptions like disputes over the human rights issue.

WHAT CHINA EXPECTS IN THE SECOND ASIA-EUROPE MEETING

March 1996 saw the first Asia-Europe Meeting bringing together heads of government from some Asian countries and the European Union for the first time. Premier Li Peng led the Chinese delegation, and a vast Chinese public watched some emotional scenes on the television during the meeting. The

Chinese press applauded the meeting because the Asian nations, many of which were once European colonies (China itself suffered from European imperialists), were now sitting around the same table with their European partners on equal footing, discussing the subjects both sides were interested in. From the Chinese perspective, this was a successful meeting, if only because this was the first of its kind. China certainly hoped that this was one of the significant steps towards helping Chinese integration into the international community, and the Chinese media evaluated it as 'a historic creation, which has strengthened mutual understanding, enhanced consensus, increased mutual trust, and promoted cooperation'.[11]

Another achievement of the first meeting, from the Chinese perspective, was a series of sincere talks between the Chinese leaders and a number of heads of states, which played a role in promoting communication, something China really needed, especially in terms of China's relations with the EU. This made the meeting effective with practical utility.

Although the first meeting did not set up a practical agenda, it did lay a good foundation for 'promoting and developing a new type of partnership between Asia and Europe' as indicated by the Chairman's Statement. It promised to promote economic and other cooperation, in addition to enhancing political dialogue. The second meeting, which will be held in London in April 1998 clearly points to the desire of all the concerned parties to continue this process. As in the first meeting, China is likely to actively take part in the second one with the expectation that the meeting will focus on more substantial matters.

1. Trade is one of the most important elements both Asia and the EU are concerned about. The trade volume between Asia (excluding Japan) and the EU may have already exceeded that between the EU and the US; with Japan included, it would far exceed the latter. For Asia, the EU is the second largest market, next to the US, and it is growing fast. There are huge stakes, but the framework is not yet shaped out. On this part, China might be among the most enthusiastic countries for an acceptable and feasible trade framework in which the current trade regionalism would not become harmful to the development of the national economy. In the meantime, China strongly opposes unilateral trade sanctions and threatening to use trade as a means to deal with political issues as seen in the Sino-US trade relations. China seems to be more confident in its trade relations with the EU, though what impact the single market and currency would have on China's trade with the EU, especially China's exports, is yet to be evaluated. In an interview with a journalist of *The Financial Times* of Britain on 24 June 1996, Chinese Premier Li Peng suggested that 'in economic exchanges, political interference from the EU was much less than from the US. The US frequently threatens to impose sanction on China in order to politicize trade and other economic affairs. That has made Chinese enterprises always

worry about the prospect of making deals with American enterprises precisely because they are never sure whether or when the US Government will pull political factors into trade issues'. The Premier personally wishes to see some change in this respect.[12] On the contrary, this problem seems much less serious in Sino-EU trade relations.

The Chinese market is vast and competitive with enormous potential, particularly in its huge need for building up infrastructure in the forthcoming years. China is also accelerating the pace of restructuring its trade system and liberalizing its trade practice so as to pull the nation's external trade on the proper track in accordance with the international norms. China welcomes European enterprises to enter the Chinese market with their advanced technology and business competitiveness. China is not a mercantilist country, but this does not mean that it should neglect making more efforts to export its manufactured goods, for it enjoys comparative advantages. China opposes protectionism, and is expected to reduce its trade barriers in the coming years if it really wants to promote trade with the developed nations. Relevant actions have been carried out as scheduled by Chinese President Jiang Zeming at the APEC Osaka meeting in Japan in 1995. There has been a large cut in China's tariffs, which will continue in order to promote free trade within the region and in the world at large. China should not have worries about this prospect. After all, viewed from the comparative advantages, China could become a manufacturing giant. China has faith that more effective Asia-EU relations will be helpful in building up a workable framework between Asia and the EU as it has been done among the APEC countries to promote trade. China would like to play a positive role in the process. China certainly expects that such a framework will consolidate and even stimulate China's trade with the EU.

2. That newly emerging Asian nations have provided a large-scale market for investment is expected to be one of the major issues in the second Asia-Europe Meeting. According to the World Bank, over the last four or five years, China has become the largest recipient country of foreign investment among the developing countries. This has been a very significant element in terms of China's economic take-off. However, due to a variety of reasons, compared to other developed nations, the EU's investment in Asia is yet far behind. How to promote the EU's investment is something Asian nations including China are particularly concerned about. Whether the second Asia-Europe Meeting would work out some substantial measures in this respect remains to be seen. But before that, the status quo, prospect and necessary measures could be carefully studied, and a task force consisting of both Asian and European scholars could be established, so that concrete proposals could be raised to the meeting for further discussion among governmental officials. China is expected to actively participate in such a task force. After all, China is supposed to be one of the most attractive places for foreign investment, and the fact is China will continue

to implement its preferential policies that are in favour of foreign investment. China will expect progress and welcome positive steps to be adopted in the second Asia-Europe Meeting.

3. Increasing mutual understanding and enhancing political dialogue are what China believes the Asia-Europe meeting should incorporate. Asia is much different from Europe in almost every sphere. There is no effectively integrated body that could represent Asia to deal with Europe, particularly with the EU, which has been making so much progress in its integration process over the last four decades. The ASEAN is certainly upgrading its active role in regional affairs covering economic, political and security cooperation; but in terms of size, member states, economic scale, and political influence it is by no means a representative of Asia. Besides, the ASEAN itself is diversified.

But the European integration is quite a different story, and the fast pace of integration represents the most typical example of the change in nature of nation-states in the 20th century. China does not oppose this process. On the contrary, China welcomes every significant step of the process including the single market and currency, the expansion of the member states of the EU, and even the defence integration. China wishes to see a more independent EU not only in economic terms, but also in political, foreign policy and security terms, because all these developments are seen as part of the multi-polarization process of the world system. But the relatively homogenous nature of Europe's nation-states is in sharp contrast to Asia where diversity among the nations is a particularly outstanding feature. At this point, China might be seen as a unique case. Therefore, in the first place, China hopes more political dialogue will be conducted between itself and other Asian nations, and the ASEAN in particular, in order to create a favourable environment for an Asian Community. On the basis of better collaboration amongst the Asian nations, more political dialogue is expected to be one of the targets of the second Asia-Europe Meeting. This should help the EU better understand and more actively support the Asian nations' desire to promote economic growth and enhance regional cooperation under the premise of maintaining political stability. Doubtless, this is exactly China's approach in terms of its cooperation with the West, including the EU.

With regard to this issue, the question is then in what sense the EU may or may not be supportive to China's political stability. Again, in his comment on the Hong Kong hand-over, Sir Leon Brittan said, 'We in the EU have been consistent in our desire for a smooth and successful transition. We continue to believe that full respect of the "one country, two systems" approach laid out in the Joint Declaration and the Basic Law is the way forward'.[13] In China's understanding, full respect should certainly include respect of the system in mainland China. It is not a one-way track. From the Chinese perspective, keeping on the political system in mainland China that is the core of 'one country' is the essence of the approach, and on the Chinese part, it means that the nation will continue to implement the practice introduced by Deng Xiaoping of building up socialism with Chinese characteristics, and that other countries, especially those of the West, should not interfere with it. As the China National People's Congress stated on 23 May 1997, 'Only on the basis of mutual respect and non-interference into each other's internal affairs can Sino-European relations move ahead',[14] pointing to the European Parliament's invitation to Taiwan's 'Foreign Minister' John Chang to address the Parliament in Strasbourg on May 22. It seems that events like this will not cease in the near future, but it is clear that they could not possibly promote political relations between China and the EU, and it would even hurt economic relations. Therefore, China sincerely believes that political dialogues are really needed, and mutual understanding must be improved. Political divergence is unavoidable, but such divergence is the product of a different historical development. It does not tell who is right and who is wrong. Neither side is qualified as the other side's teacher, nor does either side really need a teacher. The EU's increasing attention to Asia is welcomed by the Asian countries including China, not because the EU is politically superior but because it is seen as an expression of the new political reality in the post-Cold War era. There are chances to promote politically mutual understanding in the international forums like the APEC, ASEM, and ASEAN Regional Forum. Whether the second Asia-Europe Meeting will contribute to the progress in this respect remains to be seen, but China's political will is likely to continue to support the meeting with the belief that, only by active participation can genuine progress be made which will be in the interest of all parties concerned.

4. In security areas, there is the full awareness that Asia lacks a reliable multilateral security mechanism. Although Asia may not be able to copy the European model due to the diversity of the nations in the region, the European practice conveys quite a positive experience to Asia. Now, consensus is emerging among Asian nations that the region will nevertheless require some kind of multilateral system to deal with relevant issues left over by history. China has been actively taking its part in the process. The Asia-Europe Meeting provides Asia with a good opportunity to involve the EU in building up a feasible multilateral system in which China will play an important role. China expects to join efforts with other Asian nations to contribute to a more stable and prosperous Asia. In the process, China hopes that the EU would also play a positive role because it represents one of the most powerful blocs in the world, and the successful practice of a multilateral security system in Europe has given valuable lessons to other regions in the world. The second Asia-Europe Meeting is thus expected to bring about some kind of practical discussion on how the enhanced exchanges between Asia and Europe could help establish a new international system in the Asia-Pacific. In a broad sense, as the EU's economic stakes in Asia are increasing, corresponding obligations will be

required. Although Asia, especially Northeast Asia, is the fastest growing area in the world, the remaining problems left over by the Cold War are still serious, and some of them might trigger off crises as proven by recent events like those in the Korean Peninsula and the Taiwan Strait, among others. Obviously, most issues are somewhat relevant to China. While the US has been and will be deeply involved in this region, the kind of role the EU could play in maintaining peace and stability there could be an attractive subject for the Asian nations and worth discussing.

5. Last but not least is the fact that China has the urgent need to diversify its external sources (be they trade, capital, and technology, or diplomacy), as the nation is in a crucially transitional stage. Apparently, China's dependence on the outside world is increasing so dramatically in its modernization process that the nation could not possibly afford to turn back into isolation, and there is no political will at all in China to do so, no matter what happens in the post-Deng era. As Mr Swaine suggests, '... This dependence constrains the Chinese Government from reversing the open-door policy without dire consequences and also makes China vulnerable to external economic pressure'.[15] This is exactly what the Chinese leadership and scholars estimated long ago, and the pressure would be more than the economic. How to handle the challenges will depend on the wisdom of the Chinese leadership. Whether enhancing its relations with major European nations should be seen as an independent variable against the US factor remains controversial, but even if the pressure from the EU is almost the same as that from the US, from the *realpolitik* viewpoint, it could not be too bad for China to pay more attention to the EU, where what China needs like technology, capital, markets, and so on are available. More importantly, China's rapid growth together with its market potential does give a good prospect for a mutually beneficial relationship between China and the EU. But all these require a political basis, which China hopes more dialogues like the Asia-Europe Meeting could help build up.

Conclusion

China has been and will continue to be an Asian power with certain global influence in the foreseeable future, which implies that China does not seek for a global role to play. What is most relevant to China therefore must be the stability and peace of the Asia-Pacific region. It is in this respect that China will face challenges in the next decade because as a regional power, it must take appropriate responsibility, but as a rising power, insofar as its current policy orientation is concerned, its concentration on domestic development might deviate its attention from the proper track. Besides, the requirement of more obligation may also cause doubts among China's neighbours.[16] This complex situation has put the nation into a position in which its behaviour will not only be closely watched, but perhaps even seen with suspicion. Nevertheless this complex situation truly reflects China's increasing integration into the Asian family, and the trend that China's role in Asia is increasingly important is irreversible so long as domestic stability of the nation is maintained. This will have two effects: first, what happens in Asia will be increasingly related to China; and second, reliable solutions to emerging issues in the region will be increasingly relevant to China's behaviour. Therefore, when further involvement of the EU in Asia has become one of the EU's strategic priorities, China may account for an even larger part, and China's relations with the EU must be one of the major parts of the whole of Asia-Europe relations.

As the Chairman's Statement of the first Asia-Europe meeting pointed out, the meeting serves as a good basis for promoting and developing new types of partnership between Asia and the EU, aiming at maintaining peace on the two continents, sustaining growth and enhancing ties between Asia and Europe. China fully supports the targets set by the first meeting because they also serve the purpose of China's policy in the foreseeable future. As a major Asian power, China will continue its contribution not only by strengthening its relations with the EU, but also by improving collaboration with its Asian partners as proven by the latest development in the ASEAN Regional Forum and relevant meetings in July 1997 in Malaysia.[17]

In the short-term, China welcomes more business cooperation and economic exchanges with the EU, particularly in the areas like investment, technology transfer, cooperation between private sectors especially for medium and small-sized enterprises, etc. Based on continuing its economic reform programmes, China will make further efforts to open its market and to liberalize its domestic business operation. China hopes that the EU will give more support to China's entry into the WTO, which will in turn help European companies get more and better access to the Chinese market. This will greatly promote economic exchanges between Asia and the EU on the whole.

In the long run, Asia-Europe relations will go far beyond mutual economic benefits. Based on more political dialogues, both sides could be further involved in other areas like the building up of regional security mechanism, arms control, disarmament, and non-proliferation, thus contributing to the formation of the new international system. Now that China has become a very special case in this process towards the new century, closer relations between Asia and Europe in which China is an important part might impose a quite positive impact. China's full support of the Asia-Europe Meeting also demonstrates the nation's active desire to participate in the international community. That kind of interaction is absolutely a very positive signal to indicate the long-term trend of the world, that is, peace and development.

Notes

1. See Roger T. Ames: 'Continuing the Conversation on Chinese Human Rights', *Ethics & International Affairs, Carnegie Council on Ethics and International Affairs* II, 1997.
2. Ibid., p. 182.
3. Xinhua News Agency, 13 June 1997, printed in the *People's Daily*, 14 June 1997.
4. For instance, Mr Yan Xuetong, 'China's Post-Cold-War Security Strategy', *Contemporary International Relations* 8, 1995, Beijing.
5. Western media seem always to look for opposite evidence to disprove the statement like in the recent American publication, *The Coming Conflict with China*, which uses this statement as the title of one of the chapters, in which the two authors regard every sign of China's defence modernization as evidence to prove China's ambition to dominate the world. This has caused enormous criticism.
6. For instance, in his report, *China: Domestic Change and Foreign Policy* (Published in 1995 by RAND), Michael Swaine has a detailed description of what is known as recently surging nationalism.
7. This is a book written by five young Chinese writers, in which they fiercely criticize the West, especially the US and Japan, accusing them of trying to contain and constrain China's development, and the authors hold a totally contemptuous view of the American values. The book very unexpectedly became a best-seller for many months.
8. *South China Morning Post*, 16 June 1997.
9. China's missile exercise in the Taiwan Strait after Mr Lee Tenghui's 'private visit' to the US is one of the disruptive factors, but the subsequent events prove that China never intended to let things go out of control and to ruin the stability of the region which is of China's greater national interests.
10. This is China's national target, as indicated by Mr Qiao Shi, President of China People's Congress, in an interview with an American journalist of *World Opinion Update* on 23 May 1997, printed in the *Liberation Daily*, 29 May 1997, Shanghai.
11. 'A New Start of Asia-Europe Relations', *The People's Daily Editorial*, 3 March, 1996, Beijing.
12. *Containing China: Myths and Realities*, p. 642, China Yanshi Publishing House, October 1996, Beijing, edited by Sun Geqin and Cui Hongjian.
13. *South China Morning Post*, 16 June 1997, Hong Kong.
14. *Beijing Review*, 9-15 June 1997, Vol. 40, No. 23, p. 6, Beijing.
15. *China: Domestic Changes and Foreign Policy*, p. 77, the RAND Publication, 1995.

16. For instance, the board trust agreement among China, Russia and the other three Central Asian nations in 1996, and the board agreement between China and Burma, etc., which caused various speculations.
17. At the Malaysia dialogue meeting between the ASEAN and China in July 1997, the ASEAN initiated a summit between the ASEAN and China, Japan and Korea by the end of the same year. Besides, China and the ASEAN reaffirmed the importance of cooperation between the two sides in a number of arenas including the APEC, the ASEM, and the UN in addition to substantial cooperation in trade, finance, staff exchanges and technology. Chinese Foreign Minister Qian Qichen said at the meeting, 'China is expecting to make common efforts with the ASEAN to establish good neighbouring and mutual trust partnership towards the 21st century'. *Liberation Daily*, 31 July 1997, Shanghai.

THE FUTURE OF THE ASEM PROCESS: WHO, HOW, WHY, AND WHAT

JÜRGEN RÜLAND

The balance sheet of Asian-European relations in the post-Second World War period is mixed. The first initiatives for interregional cooperation date back to the early 1970s when the ASEAN countries set up a coordinating committee in Brussels with the objective of establishing an institutionalized dialogue with the then EC. By the end of the decade, a formalized dialogue had developed and in 1980 a cooperation agreement was signed in Kuala Lumpur between the EC and ASEAN. Since then EU and ASEAN Foreign Ministers have met regularly at the Post-Ministerial Conferences (PMCs) in the aftermath of ASEAN's Annual Ministerial Meeting (AMM) and every eighteen months at so-called 'ministerial meetings' hosted alternately by the EU and ASEAN. Yet, the relationship was more characterized by rhetoric than substance. ASEAN leaders repeatedly complained about the comparatively low priority accorded to their region by Europeans and the asymmetrical nature of a predominantly donor-recipient relationship. Ministerial meetings were usually hardly more than noncommittal exchanges of information. ASEAN was disappointed with the trade preferences granted by the EC, protectionism in fields such as agriculture, textiles and garments, the low level of European investment in Southeast Asia and limited technology transfers. It could, however, count on reliable European support for the annual resolutions of the UN General Assembly condemning the Vietnamese invasion of Cambodia, just as Europeans and the West could count on ASEAN support in the Afghanistan debates. Relations with Japan and China were also established in the 1970s and 1980s, but also lacked a dynamic dimension and, until the early 1990s, were better described as diplomatic rituals.[1]

Euro-Asian relations deteriorated after Tiananmen and the end of the Cold War. Freed from the Cold War necessities of courting authoritarian but pro-Western regimes, Europeans introduced a policy of conditionalities linking trade and aid with democracy, human rights, development-orientedness, market economy, disarmament and environmental protection. As a result, the ninth and tenth ASEAN-EU ministerial meetings in Luxembourg (1991) and Manila

(1992) were marred by acrimonious debates over human rights and democracy. Singled out by European criticism was the Indonesian human rights record in the former Portuguese colony of East Timor after the Dili incident in November 1991 and ASEAN's policy of 'constructive engagement' *vis-à-vis* the Burmese State Law and Order Restoration Council (SLORC). In return, ASEAN leaders such as the outspoken Malaysian Prime Minister, Mahathir Mohamad, dismissed the new moralism of the West as neo-colonialism and interference into the internal affairs of sovereign states. European criticism helped to galvanize a pan-Asian identity based on traditional Asian values, which were declared incompatible with Western-type liberal democracy. Since then dialogue between the two sides has become even thornier, although - as a result of the protracted economic recession in Europe - the four large European countries (UK, France, Germany, and Italy) returned to a more pragmatic course after 1994. This change of attitudes paved the way for the first Asia-Europe Meeting (ASEM) held in Bangkok in March 1996. As the results of the Bangkok meeting were generally perceived positively, ASEM became synonymous with a dedicated effort to rejuvenating and reinvigorating European-Asian ties. The following statements thus seek to contribute to the ongoing search for an ASEM identity that would make the fledgling forum a meaningful player in the emerging world of interregional dialogues.

Who?

From the very beginning, participation in ASEM was a controversial issue cutting across the two camps. The format finally agreed upon for the Bangkok summit that it was a 'minimalist' solution. Europe was represented by the heads of government of the fifteen members of the EU[2] plus the commission president, Asia by the leaders of the then seven ASEAN members[3], plus China Japan and South Korea[4]. Not included were Eastern European states, Australia, New Zealand, India and Pakistan all of which keenly expressed their interest to be part of ASEM. In the meantime, the queue of potential participants has grown even longer. By the end of 1997, some twenty-five nations were knocking at the doors of ASEM, which - if admitted - would expand ASEM to a forum of more than fifty members.

With the original twenty-six members, ASEM is already an unwieldy body. Except for the fifty-two-member Organization of Security and Cooperation in Europe (OSCE), it is the largest of all existing regional and interregional dialogue forums. It is a truism that large and heterogeneous intergovernmental institutions, especially if operating on a consensus basis, are prone to struggle with inertia and inefficiencies. If ASEM is to produce results in the near future - which at least in Europe is crucial in order to avoid that the new attention for

Asia sooner or later dissipates into a post-materialistic contingency - it cannot afford to rely exclusively on the smallest common denominator.

An early enlargement would aggravate these problems, in particular, if it burdens the dialogue with additional divisions beyond the already existing fault lines in the areas of trade and values. ASEM is still under probation. Without a certain consolidation period, dangers that ASEM degenerates into a talk shop cannot be outright dismissed. As a result, a premature extension of ASEM should be avoided. ASEM should not grow before the South Korean summit in the year 2000. And even then the key criterion for enlargement should be that new members do not add new conflicts to the agenda of the grouping.

From among the numerous would-be participants, a few candidates should be singled out for specific consideration. These are:
* Australia and New Zealand;
* India and Pakistan; The Central and Eastern European countries of Poland, the Czech Republic, Hungary, Slovak Republic, Slovenia, and possibly Estonia;
* The EFTA countries; Russia; and
* Myanmar and Laos as newly admitted members of ASEAN.

Australia and New Zealand will probably be more welcomed as new members by Europeans than Asians. ASEAN, for instance, insists that geographically Australia and New Zealand are not part of Asia and therefore should not be eligible for ASEM participation.[5] Moreover, their liberal political order positions them closer to European than Asian views on issues such as democracy and human rights. They may also be closer to Europe in terms of cooperation culture. With Europeans they share a result-oriented negotiation style and a preference for institutionalization and codification, although they may be more pragmatic in their approach to achieve results. While the Europeans pursue a deductive approach which rests on voluminous treaties precisely prescribing what cooperation should achieve and how the stated objectives are to be attained, the Anglo-Pacific concept is more inductive as it settles for incremental cooperation without a detailed road map for implementation.

In recent years, Australia and New Zealand have been among the leading economic performers in the OECD. Two-way trade with Europe is substantial and growing, although as a percentage of total trade, it is a far cry from the level of the 1950s and 1960s. Even more significantly, both have developed strong economic links to the Asia-Pacific over the last two decades, which now accounts for 65 per cent of their trade. They are thus in an ideal position to serve as gateways for European firms to the region. Through strategic partnerships and joint ventures Europeans as well as the Southern Pacific countries could benefit from Asian dynamism which may be stifled only temporarily by the present financial and currency crisis.[6] However, at the same time Australians in particular worry about the large European trade surplus. Participation in ASEM is thus considered as a vital avenue to rectify the trade imbalances, which are attributed to European protectionism in the fields of agriculture and other primary goods. If admitted, Australia and New Zealand must thus be expected to step up pressures on the EU to open up the single market and - following the APEC example - embark on a strategy of open regionalism, even more so as Asia's financial turmoil is having adverse effects on the Southern Pacific economies as well. In the field of economics, the Southern Pacific positions are thus doubtless more congruent with Asian than European interests.

India and Pakistan, like the rest of South Asia, have been by-passed by the recent economic dynamism of East and Southeast Asia and the emerging networks of cooperation. Especially India, as a major regional power, is now actively searching access to the regional and interregional institutions of the Asia-Pacific. It became an ASEAN dialogue partner in 1995, is a leading member of the newly inaugurated Indian Ocean Rim Association for Regional Cooperation (IOR-ARC), and participates in the BISTEC[7] subregional grouping formed in June 1997. With its considerable industrial and technological base, its huge market potential, and continuing (though slowing) economic liberalization, India may well develop into an economic partner as attractive as China for the East and Southeast Asian tigers, as well as the EU. On the other hand, South Asian integration into the Asian-European cooperation networks may speed up economic liberalization in the region and strengthen the so far modest initiatives towards regional economic cooperation under the auspices of SAARC.[8] Greater economic dynamism in South Asia is a precondition for reducing the high poverty incidence in the region, which is by far the highest in the whole of Asia.

India is closer, in terms of values, to Europeans than many Asian participants in ASEM. However, major disagreements with Europeans as well as Asians exist in the field of security due to Indian and Pakistani failures to comply with the terms of the Nuclear Non-Proliferation Treaty (NPT) as prolonged in 1995 and their refusal to accede to the Comprehensive Nuclear Test Ban Treaty. Until recently, there were strong fears in the Asian camp that an admission of India and Pakistan would paralyse ASEM as both may be tempted to use the grouping as a stage for their protracted conflict over Kashmir. However, given the confidence-building measures on both sides since the 1970s, improving (economic) cooperation within SAARC and the reconciliatory overtures made during the celebrations of the 50th anniversary of their independence, such a scenario is now becoming less likely than a few years ago. ASEAN, in particular, is now more amenable to Indian and Pakistani participation,[9] as being part of ASEM could have restraining effects on both parties, replacing past policies of brinkmanship with constructive negotiations for a peaceful settlement.

Eastern European nations increasingly seek to get a foothold in the accelerating process of economic globalization. Until now their trade policies are heavily biased towards the European market. However, despite association treaties with the EU, they still face trade obstacles in the areas of agriculture and other protected industries. Moreover, as negotiations for full EU-membership take time, expansion of trade to Asia and Asian investments in Eastern Europe will probably help to increase their international competitiveness and thus facilitate their entry into the EU. While for the Europe of fifteen, successful trade diversification of their eastern neighbours into Asia and Asian investments flowing into Eastern Europe will create additional competition. Continued economic growth and rising prosperity in Eastern Europe is a vital precondition for a smooth transformation process and the decline of regional disparities. For Asians the inclusion of Eastern European states into ASEM may be attractive because it supports their own strategies of trade diversification.[10] So far, much of ASEAN trade with Eastern Europe seems to be channelled through German intermediaries. Hence, in the long run, admission of the more advanced transformation countries to ASEM will provide a win-win situation for all parties concerned.

Remaining EFTA members (Switzerland, Norway, Iceland, and Lichtenstein) also qualify for participation in ASEM. That they are rarely named as candidates must be attributed to the fact that over the years EFTA has increasingly degenerated into a waiting room for EU membership and thus has lost much of its bargaining power. Although EFTA members are highly developed economies, small market size and referenda rejecting accession to the EU (Norway, Switzerland) deprive them of a powerful lobby among present ASEM participants. In fact, admission of EFTA members would inflate European membership in ASEM and create undue asymmetries without offering major opportunities. As EFTA members are already well integrated into the world economy, advanced Eastern European transformation economies should get priority over EFTA countries for future ASEM membership.

Russia has also been mentioned as a potential participant. However, a Russian entry would overstretch ASEM, carrying with it a baggage of problems: an uneasy relationship with Japan, disagreements with Europeans over NATO and EU extension to Eastern Europe, internal instabilities and a series of armed conflicts at its peripheries. Being a European as well as an Asian nation, it would be unclear on which side Russia would enter the dialogue. With China, India, and Russia as heavyweight members, ASEM's initiators would gradually be sidelined and the dialogue would increasingly be turned into a platform for big power politics. For the time being, Russia is better engaged through other mechanisms such as the Partnership for Peace, OSCE,

ARF, a cooperation treaty with NATO and perhaps a future Northeast Asian security mechanism.

Another delicate issue, which needs urgent attention, is how new members of regional component organizations of ASEM such as the EU and ASEAN should be treated. The issue has acutely surfaced on ASEM's agenda with the admission of Burma (Myanmar) and Laos to ASEAN in July 1997. While admission of Laos does not pose problems, a war of words erupted over Burma. Sharp European criticism of Burma's human rights record and sanctions imposed on the SLORC have been rejected by ASEAN as European interference in the organization's internal decision-making process and bolstered ASEAN's otherwise fragile solidarity with the SLORC.[11] Unfortunately, hardening positions of both sides are now increasingly threatening to derail ASEM. While Europeans tend to overlook the limited political space available to ASEAN in the extension issue which is - although few ASEAN diplomats would openly admit - clearly part of a balancing act against further Chinese advances into Burma (and other parts of Indochina), an uncompromising ASEAN stance would strengthen those voices in Europe which argue that, in the light of Asia's present economic problems, the need for intensified cooperation has lost its persuasiveness. The controversies surrounding Burmese participation in the EU-ASEAN dialogue and ASEM support two conclusions:
* There should be no automatic extension of ASEM in case regional organizations under its umbrella admit new members;
* There is a need for a temporary membership moratorium in ASEM similar to that of APEC after the Bogor summit in 1994.

This should be an acceptable compromise. ASEAN, for instance, did not try to push through Vietnam as an APEC member as long as the moratorium was in force, even though Vietnam was admitted as a new member of ASEAN in July 1995. Through an ASEM membership moratorium, the divisive Burma issue could be shelved, while the forum would be enabled to develop an identity, consolidate its procedures, achieve progress in uncontroversial areas and thus inculcate in members the certainty that ASEM is a useful interregional cooperation mechanism.

If, after the expiration of the admission moratorium, the key criterion for extension is to avoid members which introduce new lines of conflict to ASEM, the order of admission should be: Australia and New Zealand, followed by the advanced Eastern European transformation economies (Poland, the Czech Republic, and Hungary). Although India and Pakistan do not fully fit the above-mentioned criterion, their *détente* and benefits for all parties concerned justify future integration into ASEM.

How?

For a large body such as ASEM, the key problem is to ensure a maximum of efficiency with a minimum of costs and bureaucracy. The present 'laundry list' format stands for a certain degree of informality, flexibility and cost-effectiveness, but raises doubts as to what extent it will enable ASEM to move beyond short-term goals such as an increase in trade and a more intensified process of high-level government interaction. If ASEM is meant to live up to the more ambitious objectives of creating a comprehensive Asian-European partnership, several imperatives need to be considered.[12]

First, as has been suggested in the previous paragraph, there should be a moratorium on new members until 2000.

Second, for a transitory period, in order to create transparency and to facilitate a later entry, nations interested in being admitted should be given observer status. An observer status could also be contemplated for the secretaries general (or another representative in case there is no secretary general) of interregional, regional and subregional organizations which overlap with ASEM such as APEC, ASEAN, (SAARC, after India and Pakistan are admitted), IOR-ARC, BISTEC, EFTA and CEFTA (after admission of Visegrad states).[13] Moreover, applicants for membership should be immediately admitted to ASEM's subsidiary institutions such as the Asia-Europe Business Forum (AEBF) and the Asia-Europe Foundation (ASEF).

Third, instead of the present, somewhat arbitrary project list and in order to organize cooperation in a more systematic way, task forces with clear responsibility and concrete working programmes for a given time frame, should be created. Such task forces could be set up for the following policy fields:
* trade liberalization;
* investment promotion;
* financial and currency issues;
* debt management;
* security cooperation;
* infrastructure development and transportation;
* environment;
* regional development;
* human resources development;
* cultural cooperation;
* and civil society involvement.

The task forces should not only be composed of government officials, but (where possible) also of business, academic and NGO representatives. Member states would participate in the task forces on a voluntary basis. Not every member state must be represented in every working group. Members should rather concentrate their efforts on those committees where they are able to make meaningful contributions. Chairing and convenorship for the task forces would rotate among member countries biannually and coterminous with the summit schedule. For fact-finding and the formulation of policy options, the task forces should collaborate with think-tanks, academic institutions and private consultancies. The task forces should have the capability to absorb input from the emerging track-two processes and societal groups interested in the respective policy field. The task forces would thus constitute the nucleus of an increasingly decentralized epistemic community with a stake in improved Asian-European relations.

Fourth, the task forces should be coordinated by a small secretariat. The secretariat could be located in Bonn. Due to the move of the Federal Ministries to Berlin, Bonn offers ample and adequate office space and, designated by the German government as a North-South centre and a centre of sciences, provides an excellent infrastructure for an ASEM secretariat.

Fifth, summits and foreign ministers' meetings would be entrusted with monitoring and evaluating the task forces' progress, considering their policy proposals, translating them into updated work programmes and formulating new visions and targets. Moreover, leaders' meetings would have the crucial function of producing the political will for sustained progress of ASEM.

Sixth, the litmus test for the leaders' commitment to ASEM is their willingness to regularly allocate a budget to ASEM activities. So far, at least on the European side there seems to be an inclination to concentrate on those activities that can be conducted at minimal or no costs. A good case in point is the initially lacklustre commitment of funds to ASEF.[14]

These suggestions would create an ASEM of concentric circles, which would less rely on the ministerial level than on task forces, track-two processes, epistemic communities and, hopefully, broader sections of society. The earlier ASEM looses its elitist, top-heavy character, and develops a decentralized format - based on the subsidiarity principle as proposed by Gerald Segal (1997), the better.

WHY?

Answers concerning the 'why' of ASEM come from a theoretical as well as a practical level. Both are closely interlinked.

At the theoretical level, the international system witnesses a diversification of policy-making layers. At present there is a hierarchy of at least five major levels:
* the multilateral, global level;
* the interregional level;

* the regional level;
* the subregional level, and
* the conventional bilateral level.

From among the five, region-based interactions (layers two to four) are becoming increasingly crucial for international relations, while global multilateral forums and bilateral relations are losing importance. Due to a persistently growing number of states and other international actors (regimes, international and transnational organizations), their heterogeneity of interests, and the growing complexity and technicity of policy matters, consensus building at multilateral global forums is becoming increasingly difficult. Especially the crucial search for rules is a time-consuming, tiresome and costly process dominated by the smallest common denominator, while at the same time leaving players relatively powerless to deal with phenomena such as free riding and cheating. The predicament of multilateral negotiations is thus perhaps best illustrated by their protracted nature. It takes years to reach multilateral agreements such as under the Uruguay Round of GATT, the UN Convention of the Sea, a Comprehensive Nuclear Test Ban Treaty or the reform of the UN system. Other multilateral negotiations such as the debate over a New Economic World Order in the 1970s summarily broke down. If, after seemingly endless negotiations, solutions have finally been reached, the international community is faced with bothering implementation problems because frequently these agreements are shaky formula compromises, only thinly glossing over otherwise highly divergent interests. As a result, some countries either refuse to ratify them or - in order to buy time to adjust to the new regulations - take time for doing so (so that by the time of ratification they may have already become obsolete) or just ignore them, returning to opportunistic unilateral actions.

At the lower end of the hierarchy, bilateral political interactions are likewise losing importance, as more and more policy issues transcend national borders and increasingly have global, or at least regional, implications.

At the level of region-based interactions, interregional dialogues are a novelty in international policy making. ASEM is one of these emerging interregional dialogues, although governments still reject the notion of ASEM being a bloc-to-bloc forum and rather prefer a formula describing ASEM as a forum of individual countries. While the latter formula may be a convenient rhetorical device to side-step disagreements between the blocs, the various caucuses on both sides preceding the Bangkok summit and the extension discourse clearly shows that ASEM is clearly heading towards an interregional forum. At present, two forms of interregionalism may be distinguished:

* Bilateral interregionalism such as the EU-ASEAN, EU-MERCOSUR, EU-SADC, ASEAN-MERCOSUR, ASEAN-SADC, ASEAN-South Pacific Forum, ASEAN-Closer Economic Relations,[15] etc., dialogues, and
* Supraregional interregionalism as exemplified by APEC, IOR-ARC and ASEM.

At least seven major arguments can be drawn from the emerging literature on interregionalism as to why the ASEM process should be developed.[16]

1. In contemporary international relations, balance of power systems of nation-states will be increasingly complemented and, in the long run, perhaps even replaced by balance of power systems at the regional and interregional levels. ASEM can be considered as a part of such balancing regional configurations. Its creation must be seen against the background of a well-established transatlantic relationship and a more recent, however dynamically developing transpacific dialogue. In this context, ASEM provides the missing link in the triad consisting of East Asia, North America and Europe. It is thus an institution designed to balance the US which, due to its function as the hub of the two existing interregional legs, hitherto enjoyed a superior position in the triad. But far from being a merely defensive anti-American device, ASEM provides an incentive for Americans to remain engaged in Asia as well as in Europe, and even step up efforts to cooperate with both regions in order to maintain its strategic position. ASEM - if working properly - could thus unleash a spiral of mutual engagement among the major players of the triad.

2. Besides being a new element in the international power equation, ASEM (and other emerging interregional dialogues) may contribute to the institutionalization of international relations. In order to be effective, a clearing of positions is needed at the regional level, necessitating closer intraregional cooperation. The caucuses of European and the Asian members prior to the Bangkok summit are a good case in point. The EU, for instance, has to reconcile at least three major cleavages in its Asia policy: pragmatic versus value-based foreign policy, protectionist versus open trade policies, and supranational versus national security policies.[17] Moreover, implementation of the results of previous and the preparation of forthcoming meetings gives rise to the emergence of new working groups, track-two dialogues and epistemic communities, creating new channels of communication, information and interaction.

3. In line with the thoughts developed above, and taking into account the increasing number of international actors, the growing complexity and the transnational ramifications of many policy issues, interregional dialogues such as ASEM may increase the efficiency of international decision making. Previously, many of the issues discussed at the interregional level would have been raised at the global, multilateral level. By coordinating and adjusting

divergent regional positions, interregional dialogues may serve as a clearinghouse for multilateral, global forums. Their overburdened agenda may thus be streamlined and bottlenecks at the top level of the international system kept in check. However, this is not a unilinear development. As interregional dialogues also provide additional playing fields to international actors, increasing their policy options (because objectives can be pursued in different arenas), ASEM's and other interregional dialogues' rationalizing effects on international relations may be reduced or even offset.

4. ASEM offers an additional network for the integration and engagement of large powers with potential hegemonial ambitions and binding them by international agreements. ASEM could adopt such a function for China and - if enlarged - possibly also for India.

5. Interregional dialogues such as ASEM increase the chances for small and medium powers to influence international decision making. This chance is minimal in global forums which are usually dominated by big powers.

6. Interregional dialogues such as ASEM may help soften value clashes and ideological confrontations. Participants looking for benefits from such a forum will tone down disagreements over values. Although the much-debated 'Asian values' are - the way they are propagated - more a multipurpose ideological tool in the hands of ruling elite than real, ASEM is a forum where different political cultures can meet and compete in a non-confrontational way.

7. Interregionalism may open opportunities to overcome 'discriminatory regionalism' of the European type by concluding free trade agreements between regional organizations. Regions thereby adopt the function of 'new economic units' (Thiel 1997:8). Examples are interregional free trade agreements such as those between the EU and EFTA, EU and MERCOSUR, and - if some utopian thoughts are permitted - in a more distant future also between the EU and APEC or between the EU and the EAEC countries.

At a practical policy level, for Europeans the rationale for ASEM has been very clear from the outset. Economic recession at home and a sense of lost opportunities in the world's (until recently) most dynamic growth region have been the main incentives for forging closer relations with Asia. Europeans also regard ASEM as a platform for discussing with Asians a whole range of issues contested in the WTO: the social clause, protection of patents and intellectual property, a global investment code, public procurement, bidding and contract awarding procedures and the removal of alleged structural impediments on the Japanese market.

Moreover, in a world characterized by 'complex interdependence' (Keohane/Nye 1977), security cannot be treated in isolation from developments even in geographically distant regions. Europeans share with Asians interests in security-related fields such as nuclear non-proliferation, control over arms build-up and arms trade, energy supply,[18] confidence-building measures, international peacekeeping, and the restructuring of the UN. Europeans are confident that their Cold War-tested institutionalist approaches to conflict resolution can make a major contribution to security in a region where realist views of international politics are still predominant (Rüland 1995, Segal 1997). Motivations on the Asian side are more diverse, although here, too, economic interests top the agenda. Despite sluggish economic growth and a declining share in Asia's trade, Europe is still a major market for Asian products (Machetzki 1996:166-168).[19] In the face of the stuttering Asian export machine,[20] the present financial turmoil in Asia, the imminent introduction of a single European currency and forthcoming enlargements of the EU, Europe will graduate to a higher level in the foreign policy priorities of Asian countries. Asians fear that with the deepening and widening of the EU, Europe may become even more inward-looking than in the past. In view of the widely shared belief in Europe that Asia is a serious competitor for trade, jobs and investments, Asia searches for leverages to counteract deepening protectionist sentiments in the Union - especially as the latter may intensify once the weaker economies of Eastern Europe have become full-fledged members and a completed Economic and Monetary Union (EMU) forbids economic adjustments through currency devaluation and lowering of interests.[21] ASEAN fears of a 'fortress Europe' are exacerbated by moves of the European Commission gradually to phase out tariff concessions for Asian countries.[22] Taking into account that in 1992 some 72 per cent of Asian exports to the EU were covered by the EC's GSP scheme, the withdrawal of these concessions will certainly be felt by Asian exporters.[23] With intensifying competition over export markets, the EU's antidumping policy is another bone of contention which Asian countries seek to remove. An Asian camp enlarged by economic and political heavy-weights such as Japan, China and South Korea has much more bargaining power than if Asian countries individually or ASEAN alone would negotiate these issues with Brussels.

Similarly threatening for Asian economic interests are particularistic interregional and bilateral free trade agreements like those envisioned or already concluded by the EU with MERCOSUR,[24] Mexico,[25] Mediterranean countries,[26] Eastern Europe, Russia, and South Africa,[27] although ASEAN has actively begun to counter these moves by developing its own ties with Latin American, Southern African, South Pacific and Eastern European countries. The signing of a Transatlantic Agenda in December 1995, including proposals for a more intensive political dialogue and closer economic collaboration under a future TAFTA, further add to Asian concerns (Weidenfeld/Wessels 1997:149).[28] Regular consultations and closer relations would thus provide Asians with a forum to influence European trade policies in favour of an open system. The Republican victory at the congressional mid-term elections in the United States in November 1994, the rise to political prominence of figures such as former presidential candidate Ross Perot and publicist Patrick Buchanan, and fears of an imminent American return to isolationism, have additionally impressed on Asians the need for a greater diversification of interregional relations.

Equally important under the conditions of economic globalization is the continued flow of investments and technology to Asia. As European investment levels are still low compared to the United States, Japan, and East Asian NIEs, Asians expect to benefit from plant relocation and increased attention paid to Asian markets by European firms. Finally, China expects that through the softer European approach, ASEM could be used as a leverage to accelerate its entrance into the WTO on more favourable terms than the US is willing to concede to (Eglin 1997).

WHAT?

The nascent ASEM process has generated a plethora of ideas on how to strengthen Asian-European cooperation. The EU Commission published a strategy paper on Asian-European relations in 1994 and policy documents on relations with Japan, China, India and ASEAN. Following the German example, several EU member countries drafted national Asia concept papers. The Forum of Venice,[29] the ASEAN-Europe Eminent Persons Group[30] and a string of ASEM-related publications[31] also came out with numerous useful project proposals designed to give life to Asia-Europe cooperation. The work programme agreed upon in Bangkok adopted some of these proposals, raising expectations for concrete achievements in the not so far future. Most of these ideas are viable and sound. As the brainstorming stage of ASEM is over, there is a diminishing need for new spectacular policy proposals. For the London summit, no additional 'laundry lists' of projects need to be prepared. Much more important now are ingenuity, funding and organizational skills to implement the ideas that are on the table. In fact, the success of Asian-European relations does not so much hinge on innovative strategies but rather on intensity, continuity, commitment and cultural empathy.

There is not only need for more empathy in Asian-European relations, the intensity of cooperation must also increase considerably, if ASEM is to become an irreversible process. So far ASEM is characterized by an elitist approach dominated by government leaders, senior officials, spokesmen of powerful private sector associations and a few academics, but with little resonance in the wider society and - at least in Europe - very little attention by the media. Cooperation must go beyond the present pilot project character as quickly as possible and develop a certain routine and normalcy. Euro-Asian cooperation must become a normal process - as normal as transatlantic or perhaps even intra-European relations. It must consolidate in a way that, when international attention shifts to other regions and other issues in a fast-changing world, it will not fall victim to newly emerging priorities.

Taking into account these rather general suggestions and a broad spectrum of existing policy proposals, a few thoughts on further action may suffice here.

1. Top-level meetings such as the ASEM Summit in London and the Foreign Ministers' Meetings should concentrate on the essentials of Asian-European relations. Essentials are areas where both sides benefit. Taking into account the economic situation in both regions - stagnation and recession in Europe, and unprecedented, yet vulnerable growth in Asia (as shown by the present currency problems) - economic interests, at least for the time-being, must be at the centre of the process. Economic cooperation should not be derailed by acrimonious debates and publicity stunts for home audiences over values such as human rights and democracy. As top leaders only meet intermittently and the time available for summits is scarce, they should concentrate on the feasible. Confrontational value debates do not only spoil the atmosphere of summits, they also erode the good will for compromise solutions in areas where tangible benefits for both sides are in reach. Therefore, value issues should be transferred to a still nascent Euro-Asian track-two process where these controversial issues could be discussed frankly without the danger of damaging official relations. To this end, an intellectually lively track-two process should be placed on firm foundations.[32]

This, of course, does not mean that the EU should sacrifice the normative base of its foreign policy. There is no question that in cases of blatant human rights violations appropriate European action is called for. But the EU should also note that - with the exception of Burma (and increasingly Cambodia) - there have been considerable improvements in the observation of human rights in the region over the last two decades. They are documented in the annual reports of international human rights organizations such as Amnesty International.[33] Therefore, a more sophisticated approach to deal with value issues is needed. Greater sophistication in the value debate would also help to overcome the EU's internal policy disagreements and the resultant myopic zigzag policy between *realpolitik* and moralism and between principles and embarrassing opportunism (Rüland 1996:62). Any change of government in Europe entails the likelihood of a major policy shift with respect to democracy and human rights. The reaffirmed emphasis on values by the newly installed British Labour Government is a good case in point. Predictably the admonitions of Southeast Asian leaders by British Foreign Minister Robin Cook during his Southeast Asia tour in August 1997, have caused new irritations in EU-ASEAN relations, placed new obstacles in the way of the consolidation of ASEM and complicated the formulation of a European Asia policy. A similar policy shift must be expected in Germany if the Social Democrats win the elections in

1998. If the EU's Common Foreign and Security Policy cannot be employed to help in silencing the cacophony of policy statements, the EU's Asia policy will never fully develop its potential. It will remain incalculable and thus always struggle with a credibility gap.

On the other hand, it must be clearly stated that if Malaysian Prime Minister Mahathir's call for a redrafting of the UN Universal Declaration of Human Rights (UDHR) is reflecting ASEAN consensus,[34] and if ASEAN decides to lobby actively for such a move, value issues will lead to a head-on collision in high-level meetings and bring the nascent cooperation to a grinding halt. Failure of the Asian side to recognize that there is a firm consensus in European (and, in general, Western) societies that tinkering with the UDHR is taboo, would undermine the position of all those in Europe working for a closer (and, at the same time, more pragmatic) Asian-European relationship.

2. The EU's development aid provided to Asian countries is substantial. It is only exceeded by Japan, but is almost three times higher than American aid. Much of European aid is devoted to poverty alleviation in backward rural areas. However, with increasing prosperity, other Asian NIEs must participate in these efforts. From a European perspective, the Asian credo that market forces will create the magic of developing lagging regions such as the Indochinese peninsula, is unacceptable. What in practice is behind the market forces are resource-depleting projects in the extractive sector or large-scale infrastructure projects. If the burden sharing is such that Asian investments in these subregions are primarily used for laying the foundations for an economic head start, while the rest of the international donor community is responsible for curing the environmental disasters and the adverse social concomitants of a merely growth-oriented development strategy, it needs serious reconsideration. The present incongruities are perhaps well illustrated in the following two figures: while only 12 per cent of European development aid to Asia has commercial relevance,[35] fast-growing Asian nations such as South Korea spend an abysmally low 0.05 per cent of their GDP for development aid.[36]

3. It would be a great mistake if the current troubles of some Asian economies would prompt Europeans to scale down their efforts for better Asian-European relations. A genuine desire to improve relations leaves no room for *schadenfreude*[37] and the repayment of what was considered by Europeans as growing Asian hubris in the light of fabulous economic growth rates. In fact, the present crisis should be part of the agenda of the London summit and Europeans should offer their Asian counterparts an aid package that complements those of the International Monetary Fund (IMF), the Asian Development Bank (ADB) and individual countries such as the US and Japan. More than anything else, this would drive home the message to the Asian side that Europe's new Asia policy means business and is more than an opportunistic move to improve its position within the triad.[38] It must not

necessarily be 'tough love' that East Asians need, but Gerald Segal is right when he argues that it is in times of crisis that key relationships are formed.[39] The enduring transatlantic relationship is the best example.

4. The top-heavy and somewhat sterile nature of Asian-European relations can only be overcome when they involve civil society. Speaking in Brussels, Singaporean Prime Minister, Goh Chok Tong, proposed a three-staged process towards this end.[40] According to Mr Goh, initial work is to be done by think-tanks and expert groups in order to close the knowledge gap and to create better mutual understanding, thus laying the foundations for civil society to come in at the third and last stage. I agree with the substance of Mr Goh's proposals, except for the timing. Civil society must be involved from the very beginning. If the Asia-Europe dialogue remains for a considerable period a top-heavy process in the exclusive circles of high-ranking government officials, the academe, and think-tanks, ASEM projects will face great difficulties at the implementation stage. Even the brightest ideas are bound to fail, if they are not properly understood at the grass-roots level. By 'grass-roots level', I mean local and regional governments, national government field offices, the universities and other educational institutions, the local chambers of commerce and business associations as well as the local media. What sense does it make if, for instance, the ASEM Summit agrees on a substantial expansion of student exchange, but local immigration offices in one or several EU member states block student mobility by a mixture of red tape and ill will encouraged by highly restrictive immigration laws? What if rectors and university administrators feel that European universities are already overcrowded and thus are not prepared to take students from Asia? What if governments send business delegations to Asia, but SMEs and local business associations fail to respond to such initiatives? These examples are not fiction, they have real backgrounds.

Involving civil society in the process is thus one of the most urgent tasks for ASEM. One important field with a potential for multiple effects is cultural cooperation - which Wim Stokhof has called the 'third dimension of Asian-European relations' (Stokhof 1997). While Mr Goh sets great hopes in the dialogue of experts, Europeans only slowly realize that they increasingly lack congenial counterparts on the Asian side. Under their new Asia policies, Europeans make great efforts to attract Asian scientists and engineers to their universities because they rightfully regard them as their business partners of tomorrow. It cannot be denied that such a policy makes sense for both sides - for the less advanced Asian countries eager to close the technology gap as well as for European manufacturers. From a European perspective, it is, however, worrisome that there is a rapidly declining number of social scientists and economists coming to Europe for advanced studies.[41] The overwhelming majority of the Asian think-tank elite is - if not trained at home - educated in

North America and thus views many issues through an American lens. As a result, the know-how of Asian decision makers about Europe has been constantly on the decline. A promising attempt to bridge this knowledge gap are the European Studies programmes such as the one existing for more than seven years at the National University of Singapore or the recently opened master's programme at Bangkok's Chulalongkorn University. However, this is only a beginning; much more joint research between Asian and European scholars on Europe is needed and more Asian scholars should be invited for teaching in European universities.

Media is another crucial area for multiplying knowledge and informing society about the other side. Many reports in Asian newspapers about Europe are authored by European journalists. While European journalists rightfully see their watchdog function as a noble cause of their profession, critical reports may be misread by audiences not accustomed to hard-hitting analyses and thus contribute to the increasingly negative image Europe is facing in parts of Asia. On the other hand, few Asian journalists are European specialists. The EU is usually not even covered by a correspondent residing in Brussels, but one responsible for the whole of Europe based in London, Paris or Bonn. Vice versa, the European media, too, lack sophistication when reporting about Asia. The tendency to report in an *ad hoc*ist way and to concentrate on the three big 'Cs' - calamities, coups, and crises - has repeatedly been criticized by Western and even more frequently by Asian observers. Similarly deplorable, however, is the fact that, at the local level, Asia almost does not exist in European media. Yet, especially newspapers with local circulation are the main source of information for the small and medium-scale entrepreneur we would like to see doing business with Asia and the immigration officer who handles the visa applications of Asian students. Editors and journalists in the local media must thus become another prime target group for civil society involvement.

It is regrettable, in this respect, to note that the European Commission and European governments have done little to educate the wider public about the virtues of a closer Euro-Asian relationship. With perhaps the sole exception of Business Leaders' Meetings, very little has transpired through the Western media about the progress made since Bangkok. It would, for instance, be interesting to learn something about the way the Junior ASEAN-EU Managers' Programme has been received by the business communities of both sides, what activities have been initiated under Asia Urbs, or what is the present status of university cooperation and student exchange. What about the proposals formulated at the Forum of Venice to set up an Asian-European version of SOCRATES (hopefully minus the awful bureaucracy and the disappointing budget of the 'reformed' SOKRATES version)? While the Commission's delegations in Asia have done a marvellous job to provide first-class information via the Internet, the problem is that it is accessible only for those that actively seek this information. Information, however, should be brought to the public as a service, especially if the image of a product (in this case the EU) needs improvement.[42]

I have outlined more proposals elsewhere (Rüland 1996):
* The creation of Institutes of European Culture;
* The deployment of European Volunteers in the EU's Asian development projects;
* City twinning programmes linking cultural exchange with economic objectives (alternatively
* and/or additionally: twinning of subregional cooperation arrangements);[43]
* and familiarizing secondary school teachers with Asia.

There is no need to repeat them here, because many of these ideas are not unfamiliar to experts working on the improvement of Asian-European relations. Yet, summing up what has been discussed above, much more funding and organizational effort is needed for them to succeed. Only the civil society-based projects are able to create the critical mass of networks needed to make Asia-European relations a self-sustaining process. Money, mobility and multiplicators are key ingredients for their success.

REFERENCES

Algieri, Franco
1996 'Die Asienpolitik der Europäischen Union', in: Werner Weidenfeld and Bernhard Wessels (eds) *Jahrbuch Europäische Integration*, Bonn: Europa Union Verlag 1996, pp. 253-60
ASEAN-European Union
1996 *A Strategy for a New Partnership*. Report of The Eminent Persons Group
Asia Europe Forum on Culture
1996 *Values and Technology. Towards a Stronger Mutual Understanding*. Proceedings. The Forum of Venice, Venice, Giorgio Cini Foundation, 18-19 January 1996
Bridges, Brian
1992 'Japan and Europe. Rebalancing a Relationship', *Asian Survey* XXXII, No. 3, March 1992, pp. 230-45
Calder, Kent E.
1996 *Asia's Deadly Triangle. How Arms, Energy and Growth Threaten to Destabilize Asia-Pacific*, London: Nicholas Brealey Publishing
Camroux, David and Christian Lechervy
1996 'Close Encounter of a Third Kind?' The Inaugural Asia-Europe Meeting of March 1996, *The Pacific Review* 9, No. 3, pp. 442-53
Commission of the European Communities
1994 *Towards a New Asia Strategy*, Brussels, 13 July, p. 15
1996 *Creating a New Dynamic in EU-ASEAN Relations*, Brussels
Downer, Alexander
1996 'Australien, Deutschland und Europa: Eine neue Partnerschaft', *KAS Auslandsinformationen*, 12, pp. 25-35
Eglin, Michaela
1997 'China's Entry into the WTO with a Little Help from the EU', *International Affairs* 73, No. 3, pp. 489-508
European Union
1996 *The European Union and Asia*, Brussels
Godement, François
1997 'The Key to an Asia-Europe Partnership Lies in Europe', in: Paul van der Velde (ed.) *Cultural Rapprochement Between Asia and Europe. Five Essays on the Asia-Europe Relationship*, Leiden: International Institute for Asian Studies, pp. 43-52
Goh Chok Tong
1997 'The Asia-Europe Dialogue. The Road to Understanding', in: Paul van der Velde (ed.) *Cultural Rapprochement Between Asia and Europe.*

Five Essays on the Asia-Europe Relationship, Leiden: International Institute for Asian Studies, pp. 15-22
IFO Schnelldienst
1996 *EU und Asien: Wachstumsregionen zum beiderseitigen Nutzen*, Munich, No. 35
Jacquet, Pierre
1996 'The Third Leg of the Triad', *NIRA Review*, Autumn, pp. 7-10
Keohane, R.O. and J.S. Nye
1977 *Power and Interdependence. World Politics in Transition*, Boston and Toronto: Little, Brown and Company
Korte, Karl-Rudolf
1989 'Japan und der Europäische Binnenmarkt', *Aussenpolitik* 40. Jahrgang, Heft 4, pp. 407-17
Korte, Karl-Rudolf
1995 'Die Wirtschaftsbeziehungen zur EU', in: Hans-Jürgen Meyer and Manfred Pohl (eds) *Länderbericht Japan. Geographie, Geschichte, Politik, Wirtschaft, Gesellschaft, Kultur*, Darmstadt, Wissenschaftliche Buchgesellschaft
Machetzki, Rüdiger
1996 'Europas Bedeutsamkeit für Ostasien. Wider einige übliche Argumente', *Südostasien aktuell*, März, pp. 166-8
Maull, Hanns W.
1996 'Von Europa lernen? Konfliktpotentiale und die neue Sicherheitsstruktur imostasiatisch-pazifischen Raum', *Frankfurter Allgemeine Zeitung*, 12 April, p. 13
1997a 'Regional Security Cooperation: A Comparison of Europe and East Asia', *Internationale Politik und Gesellschaft* 1, pp. 49-63
1997b 'Theaterdonner im Kampf der Kulturen. Europa und die Wiederentdeckung der Wachstumsregion Asien', *Frankfurter Allgemeine Zeitung*, 3 July, p. 11
Maull, Hanns W. and Akihiko Tanaka
1997 *ASEM: The Geopolitical Dimension*, mimeographed paper
Menotti, Roberto
1995 'European-Chinese Relations in the Nineties', *The International Spectator*, XXX, No. 4, October-December
Pape, Wolfgang
1996 'Die EU und Ostasien unter besonderer Berücksichtigung der politischen und wirtschaftlichen Beziehungen zu Japan', in: Moritz Röttinger and Claudia Weyringer (eds) *Handbuch der europäischen Integration. Strategie - Struktur - Politik der Europäischen Union*, Wien: Manzsche Verlags- und Universitätsbuchhandlung, pp. 565-79

Rhein, Eberhard
1996 'Besser als ihr Ruf: die EU-Außenpolitik', *Internationale Politik* 51, No. 3, March, pp. 55-8
Rinsche, Günter
1996 'Die asiatische Herausforderung. Zum Verhältnis zwischen Europa und Asien', *KAS Auslandsinformationen* 12, pp. 3-24
Rüland, Jürgen
1995 'Politische und sozio-kulturelle Aspekte von Kooperation und Integration im asiatisch-pazifischen Raum', in: Guido Eilenberger, Manfred Mols, and Jürgen Rüland (eds) *Kooperation, Regionalismus und Integration im asiatisch-pazifischen Raum*, Hamburg: Mitteilungen des Instituts für Asienkunde, No. 266, pp. 73-92
1996 'The Asia-Europe Meeting (ASEM): Towards a New Euro-Asian Relationship?', Rostock: Rostocker Informationen zu Politik und Verwaltung
Segal, Gerald
1997 'Thinking Strategically about the Subsidiarity Question', *The Pacific Review* 10, No. 1, pp. 124-34
Sideri, Sandro
1995 'The Economic Relations of China and Asia-Pacific with Europe', *Development Policy Review.* 13, pp. 213-46
Stokhof, Wim
1997 'The Third Dimension of the Asia-Europe Relationship: Reflections on Asian and European Studies in Europe', in: Paul van der Velde (ed.) *Cultural Rapprochement between Asia and Europe. Five Essays on the Asia-Europe Relationship*, Leiden: International Institute for Asian Studies, pp. 23-32
Svensson, Thommy
1997 'Prospects for Improved Pacific Asia-European Cooperation in Research, Education, and Culture', in: Paul van der Velde (ed.) *Cultural Rapprochement Between Asia and Europe. Five Essays on the Asia-Europe Relationship*, Leiden: International Institute for Asian Studies, pp. 33-42
Thiel, Elke
1996 'Der "neue" Regionalismus in den internationalen Wirtschafsbeziehungen: Zur Bewertung regionaler Integrationsansätze im Vergleigh', in: Rolf H. Hasse (ed.) *Nationalstaat im Spagat: Zwischen Suprastaatlichkeit und Subsidiarität.* Veröffentlichung des Studienkreises Internationale Beziehungen, Bd. 6. Stuttgart, pp. 127-154

Velde, Paul van der (ed.)
1997 *Cultural Rapprochement Between Asia and Europe. Five Essays on the Asia-Europe Relationship*, Leiden: International Institute for Asian Studies

Weggel, Oskar
1996 '"ASEM": Nachhilfeunterricht für europäische Politiker in Sachen Asien', *CHINA aktuell*, February, pp. 159-61

Weidenfeld, Werner and Wolfgang Wessels (eds)
1997 *Europe from A to Z. Guide to European Integration*, Luxembourg: Office for Official Publications of the European Communities

Yeo Lay Hwee
1997 'The Bangkok ASEM and the Future of Asia-Europe Relations', *Southeast Asian Affairs 1997*, Singapore: Institute of Southeast Asian Studies, pp. 33-45

Notes

1. For an assessment of European-Japanese relations see Karl-Rudolf Korte, 'Japan und der Europäische Binnenmarkt', *Aussenpolitik*, 40. Jahrgang, Heft 4, 1989, pp. 407-17; Brian Bridges, 'Japan and Europe. Rebalancing a Relationship', *Asian Survey* XXXII, No. 3, March 1992, pp. 230-45; Karl-Rudolf Korte, 'Die Wirtschaftsbeziehungen zur EU', in: Hans-Jürgen Meyer and Manfred Pohl (eds) *Länderbericht Japan. Geographie, Geschichte, Politik, Wirtschaft, Gesellschaft, Kultur*, Darmstadt, Wissenschaftliche Buchgesellschaft 1995, pp. 337-50; Wolfgang Pape, 'Die EU und Ostasien unter besonderer Berücksichtigung der politischen und wirtschaftlichen Beziehungen zu Japan', in: Moritz Röttinger and Claudia Weyringer (eds) *Handbuch der europäischen Integration. Strategie - Struktur - Politik der Europäischen Union*, Wien: Manzsche Verlags- und Universitätsbuchhandlung 1996, pp. 565-79; on European-Chinese relations see Sandro Sideri, 'The Economic Relations of China and Asia-Pacific with Europe', *Development Policy Review* 13, 1995, pp. 213-46, and Roberto Menotti, 'European-Chinese Relations in the Nineties', *The International Spectator* XXX, No. 4, October-December 1995.
2. Absent in Bangkok were the prime ministers of Spain, Sweden, Denmark, and Luxembourg. Their countries were however represented by other prominent cabinet ministers.
3. At the 30th ASEAN Ministerial Meeting held in July 1997 in Kuala Lumpur Burma (Myanmar) and Laos were admitted as new ASEAN members, bringing ASEAN's membership to nine.

4. However, it did not go unnoticed that, incidentically or not, the Asian participants are identical with the members of the East Asian Economic Caucus (EAEC) so keenly propagated by Malaysian Prime Minister Mahathir as an organization representing East Asian interests in the emerging interregional dialogues (Camroux and Lechervy 1996, p. 448).
5. Interview information.
6. This, at least, is the opinion of Paul Krugman. See his interview with *Asiaweek* 3 October, 1997, p. 68, 'Krugman sees the light. A Top economist calls Asia's woes "solvable"'.
7. BISTEC members are countries grouped around the Andaman Sea such as Bangladesh, India, Sri Lanka and Thailand. Myanmar has observer status.
8. SAARC is the South Asian Association for Regional Cooperation. Formed in 1985 the seven-member grouping consists of Bangladesh, Bhutan, India, the Maldives, Nepal, Pakistan and Sri Lanka.
9. Interview information.
10. Examples are the Polish Southeast Asia Forum held in Warsaw in September 1996. See 'Southeast Asia builds Polish connection', *Asia Times,* 5 September, 1996, p. 4 and efforts to strengthen relations with Latin American nations. See 'Latin America, Asia to expand economic ties', *Jakarta Post,* 2 October, 1997, p. 10, 'Southeast Asia, Latin America to expand ties', *Jakarta Post,* 6 October, 1997, p. 12. Malaysia and Indonesia also are seek to improve ties with South Africa where Malaysia has already become the second largest investor. See 'ASEAN seeks to boost trade with southern Africa', *Jakarta Post,* 14 October, 1997, p. 10.
11. The Philippines and Thailand were much more reluctant to agree to an early Burmese admission to ASEAN than Singapore, Malaysia and Indonesia.
12. Already now there are voices disputing the need for a special Asia policy by arguing that European exports to Asia are growing rapidly, that Asia is still more dependent on the European and American markets than vice versa, that notions of a shifting balance of economic power to the Asia-Pacific region are premature, and that Asia's future economic growth will be seriously inhibited by growth pathologies such as environmental degradation, exhaustion of natural resources, unplanned international migration, and social and spatial inequities.
13. The EU should also actively seek observer status in APEC, IOR-ARC and BISTEC.
14. In the meantime, members have pledged some USD 25,2 million for ASEF's activities. The foundation has its headquarters in Singapore. Executive director is Prof. Tommy Koh, a former Singaporean ambassador to the UN and the US.

15. Comprising Australia and New Zealand.
16. The following arguments are mainly drawn from Rüland (1996); Maull (1997a); Maull and Tanaka (1997).
17. The third cleavage refers to the question whether, apart from the Commission, the United Kingdom and France should hold individual seats on the ARF. See Rüland (1996, p. 49).
18. On the energy and nuclear issues see Kent E. Calder (1996).
19. Especially for Asia's developing countries, Europe is still the most important market after the US. See Commission of the European Communities, *Towards a New Asia Strategy*, Brussels, 13 July, 1994, p. 15.
20. Commission of the European Communities, *Towards a New Asia Strategy*, Brussels, 13 July, 1994, p. 6.
21. See *Far Eastern Economic Review*, 3 July, 1996, p. 68.
22. See *Far Eastern Economic Review*, 6 October, 1994, pp. 15-16 and *Jakarta Post*, 12 February, 1997, p. 1.
23. Affected are India, Pakistan, Thailand, Indonesia, Malaysia and China all of which are set to see their access to the Union's preferential system cut in half for exports of such key products as textiles, garments, leather goods and fishery products. See *Jakarta Post*, 21 February, 1996, p. 9.
24. See *Jakarta Post*, 27 February, 1996, p. 5.
25. See *Handelsblatt*, 22 May, 1996, p. 3.
26. See *Handelsblatt*, 29 November, 1995, p. 11.
27. See *Das Parlament*, 26 February, 1996, p. 19; Eberhard Rhein, 'Besser als ihr Ruf: die EU-Außenpolitik', *Internationale Politik* 51, No. 3, March 1996, pp. 55-8.
28. See *Bangkok Post*, 29 February, 1996, p. 9; *Handelsblatt*, 10 May, 1996, p. 2
29. See *Asia Europe Forum on Culture, Values and Technology. Towards a Stronger Mutual Understanding. Proceedings.* The Forum of Venice, Venice: Giorgio Cini Foundation, 18-19 January, 1996.
30. See ASEAN - European Union (1996): *A Strategy for a New Partnership*. Report of The Eminent Persons Group.
31. See Rüland, Jürgen (1996): *The Asia-Europe Meeting (ASEM): Towards a New Euro-Asian Relationship?*, Rostock: Rostocker Informationen zu Politik und Verwaltung.
32. Europeans, for their part, have not yet done enough to make these track-two dialogues truly meaningful. While in some European countries laudable efforts have been undertaken to initiate dialogues with Asian decision-making and think-tank elites, it testifies to the above-mentioned lack of empathy that - at least in Germany - the political top leaders are usually

unavailable for addressing these meetings as keynote speakers. While a meeting of Asian and European security experts jointly organized by the Konrad-Adenauer-Foundation and the Institute for Security and Development Studies (ISDR) in Manila in December 1996 was addressed by Philippine President Fidel V. Ramos, Vice President Joseph Estrada, Foreign Minister Domingo Suazon and National Security Adviser Jose Almonte, there were no keynote speakers of comparable stature in the two German meetings held in Bonn in May 1995 and in November 1997. Also the organizers of a high-powered international symposium on the occasion of ASEAN's 30-year anniversary of the University of Mainz tried in vain to find a cabinet member of the state government of Rhineland-Palatinate to welcome the guests who came from Southeast Asia, Australia, the United States and several European countries. Status-related issues as these may appear unfamiliar to Europeans, but they have great meaning for Asians. For them they symbolize the priority which is accorded by the European side to these kind of exchanges. As one keen observer of Asian-European relations remarked, Europeans frequently tend to overlook the fact that politics in Asia is not only related to substance but to an almost similar extent to form as well.

33. See Amnesty International (1996): *Jahresbericht 1996*, Frankfurt a.M.: Fischer Taschenbuch Verlag.
34. As recently at the PMC of the 30th ASEAN Ministerial Meeting. See *Jakarta Post*, 1 August, 1997, p. 1 and subsequent commentaries. See *Jakarta Post*, 6 August, 1997, p. 1, 9 August, 1997, p. 1 and 16 August, 1997, p. 5.
35. See Commission of the European Communities, *Towards a New Asia Strategy*, Brussels, 13 July, 1994, p. 6.
36. See *Far Eastern Economic Review*, 17 October, 1996, p. 108
37. Moralizing newspaper articles such as the one of Helga Einecke for the Deutsche Presse Agentur (DPA) entitled 'Greed makes the tigers sick' are not particularly helpful for educating the European public on the reasons for the economic troubles in the region. See *Jakarta Post*, 21 November, 1997, p. 4.
38. For similar views see also *Asian Wall Street Journal*, 14 November, 1997, p. 10.
39. See *International Herald Tribune*, 17 November, 1997, p. 1.
40. See Goh Chok Tong, 'The Asia-Europe Dialogue. The Road to Understanding', in: Paul van der Velde (ed.) *Cultural Rapproachement Between Asia and Europe. Five Essays on the Asia-Europe Relationship*, Leiden: International Institute for Asian Studies, pp. 15-22.

41. Except, of course, the UK.
42. As corroborated by a study conducted by Research International Asia of Singapore on behalf of the European Commission in 1995. According to the study, the majority of the respondents has never seen brochures and other information material of the EU. See *Handelsblatt*, 22 June, 1998, p. 8.
43. Such as for instance, between the Four Engines for Europe (Baden-Württemberg, Lombardia, Rhone-Alpes, Catalonia) and ASEAN growth triangles such as Sijori.

ANNEXES

ANNEX 1

ASEM 1: CHAIRMAN'S STATEMENT 1996

TOWARDS A COMMON VISION FOR ASIA AND EUROPE

1. The inaugural Asia-Europe Meeting (ASEM) was held in Bangkok on 1-2 March 1996 and was attended by the Heads of State and Government from ten Asian nations and fifteen European nations with the Head of Government of Italy acting also as President of the Council of the European Union, and the President of the European Commission. The Heads were accompanied by their Foreign Ministers, Members of the Commission and other Ministers. The Prime Minister of Thailand chaired this historic Meeting.

2. The Heads of State and Government and the President of the European Commission had an audience with Their Majesties King Bhumibol Adulyadej and Queen Sirikit at the Ananta Samakhom Throne Hall on 1 March 1996.

3. The Meeting discussed a wide range of issues and provided the opportunity for the Heads to share their concerns and aspirations, and develop a common vision for the future. The Meeting recognized the need to strive for a common goal of maintaining and enhancing peace and stability, as well as creating conditions conducive for economic and social development. To this end, the Meeting forged a new comprehensive Asia-Europe Partnership for Greater Growth. This partnership aims at strengthening links between Asia and Europe, thereby contributing to peace, global stability and prosperity. In this connection, the Meeting underscored the importance for both Asia and Europe to maintain dialogue with other regions.

4. The Meeting recognized that an important goal of this partnership is for both Asia and Europe to share the responsibilities in building greater understanding between the peoples of both regions. Strengthened dialogue on an equal basis between Asia and Europe in a spirit of cooperation and through the sharing of perceptions on a wide range of issues would enhance mutual understanding and benefit both regions. The dialogue will, in view of the global implications of the major regional integration, also help ensure that such integration benefit the international community as a whole.

FOSTERING POLITICAL DIALOGUE

5. The Meeting of the Heads from Asia and Europe reflects their common desire to strengthen political dialogue. Countries of Asia and Europe should highlight and expand common ground, enhance understanding and friendship, and promote and deepen cooperation. The dialogue among the participating countries should be conducted on the basis of mutual respect, equality, promotion of fundamental rights and, in accordance with the rules of international law and obligations, non-intervention, whether direct or indirect, in each other's internal affairs. The Heads reviewed political and security situations in both regions and underlined the importance of support for international initiatives to solve outstanding problems. The Meeting also agreed to promote intellectual exchanges between the two regions in the context of fostering political dialogue.

6. The Meeting agreed on the importance of enhancing the already existing dialogues between Asia and Europe on general security issues and in particular on confidence building. Many Asian countries have established regular dialogue with the European Union. The European Union and the Asian nations have also engaged in discussions on political matters at such forums as the ASEAN-EU Dialogue, the ASEAN Regional Forum (ARF) and the ASEAN Post Ministerial Conferences (PMC).

7. The Meeting reaffirmed its strong commitment to the United Nations Charter, the Universal Declaration on Human Rights, the 1986 Declaration on the Right to Development, the 1992 Rio Declaration on Environment and Development, the 1993 Declaration of Vienna and Programme of Action of the World Conference on Human Rights, the 1994 Cairo Programme of Action of the International Conference on Population and Development, the 1995 Copenhagen Declaration on Social Development and Programme of Action, and the 1995 Beijing Declaration and Platform of Action for the Fourth World Conference on Women.

The Meeting also agreed to cooperate in promoting the effective reform and greater democratization of the UN system, including inter alia the issues concerning the Security Council, the General Assembly, the Economic and Social Council and UN finances, with a view to reinforcing its preeminent role in maintaining and promoting international peace and security and sustainable development. In this connection, the Meeting agreed to the initiation of a dialogue between representatives of participating nations of the ASEM in New York to consider the vital question of the UN reform.

8. The Meeting agreed on the importance of strengthening global initiatives on arms control, disarmament and non-proliferation of weapons of mass destruction and reaffirmed that Asian and European countries will enhance cooperation in these fields. The Meeting therefore attached particular importance to the early conclusion of the Comprehensive Test Ban Treaty in 1996. The Meeting noted that, in their efforts to contribute to the Nuclear Non-Proliferation Treaty (NPT) regime, the ten Southeast Asian countries have concluded the Southeast Asia Nuclear Weapon-Free Zone (SEANWFZ) Treaty in Bangkok in December 1995. The Leaders reiterated their determination to pursue systematic and progressive efforts to reduce nuclear weapons globally with the ultimate goal of eliminating those weapons and of general and complete disarmament under strict and effective international controls. The Meeting emphasized its commitment to the non-proliferation and prohibition of biological and chemical weapons, in particular to the early entry into force of the Chemical Weapons Convention. The Meeting supported efforts in the Conference on Disarmament to start negotiations on a fissile material cut-off on the basis of the agreed mandate.

REINFORCING ECONOMIC COOPERATION

9. The Meeting recognized the great potential for synergy between Asia and Europe on account of the economic dynamism and diversity of the two regions. Asia's emergence as an immense market has spawned great demand for consumer goods, capital equipment, financing and infrastructure. Europe, on the other hand, is a major market in the world for goods, investments and services, even more so since the completion of the Single Market. Opportunities thus exist for both regions to expand the market for goods, capital equipment and infrastructure development projects, and to increase the flows of capital, expertise and technology.

10. The Meeting recognized that the growing economic links between the two regions form the basis for a strong partnership between Asia and Europe. To further strengthen this partnership, the Meeting expressed its resolve to generate greater two-way trade and investment flows between Asia and Europe. Such a partnership should be based on the common commitment to market economy, open multilateral trading system, non-discriminatory liberalization and open regionalism. The Meeting stressed that any regional integration and cooperation should be WTO consistent and outward looking.

11. The Meeting agreed that the ASEM process should complement and reinforce efforts to strengthen the open and rules-based trading system embodied in the WTO. Full participation in the WTO by ASEM countries will strengthen the organization. Recognizing the importance of the first WTO Ministerial Conference to be held in Singapore in December 1996, the Meeting agreed that the participants from Asia and Europe would work closely together towards the success of the WTO. The Meeting agreed that a priority facing the WTO was how to ensure full implementation of commitments made in the Uruguay Round. Participants also underlined the urgent need to bring unfinished Uruguay Round negotiations to successful conclusions and to pursue the so-called built-in agenda, agreed to at Marrakesh. Asian and European participants will consult closely on new issues for the WTO agenda.

12. To promote greater trade and investment between Asia and Europe, the Meeting agreed to undertake facilitation and liberalization measures involving the simplification and improvement of customs procedures, and standards conformance. ASEM will also aim for the reduction of trade barriers to avoid trade distortion and create better market access thus encouraging greater trade flows between Asia and Europe. The Meeting underscored the urgent need to increase European investments in Asia from their present low levels, as well as to encourage Asian investments in Europe.

13. The Meeting decided to ask senior officials to convene an informal meeting at an early opportunity on ways to promote economic cooperation and in particular liberalization and facilitation of trade and investment. Initial emphasis should be placed on the WTO issues indicated above, but officials should also try to identify other measures that could be taken by ASEM countries in order to facilitate trade and investment. Officials may also look into how training programmes, economic cooperation and technical assistance could be further intensified in order to facilitate trade and investment.

14. The Meeting agreed to encourage the business and private sectors, including small and medium sized enterprises of the two regions, to strengthen their cooperation with one another and contribute to increasing trade and investment between Asia and Europe. For this purpose, the Meeting agreed to establish in due course an Asia-Europe Business Forum. Promoting Cooperation in other areas

15. The Meeting agreed that intensified science and technology cross-flows between Asia and Europe, especially in priority driving sectors such as

agriculture, information and communication technology, energy and transport, are important for strengthening the economic links between the two regions. The Meeting expressed the view that cooperation in the field of human resources development constitutes an important component of the economic cooperation between Asia and Europe. The Meeting also supported the strengthening of cooperation on all levels of education and vocational and management training. The Meeting also stressed the need to improve development cooperation between the two regions, giving priority to poverty alleviation, promoting the role of women and cooperating in the public health sector, including the strengthening of global efforts to combat AIDS and to promote AIDS prevention. The Meeting further agreed that the two regions should promote a dialogue within the ASEM on development cooperation with other regions, where feasible, sharing their respective experiences in this area.

16. The Meeting acknowledged the importance of addressing environmental issues such as global warming, protection of water resources, deforestation and desertification, biodiversity of species, and marine environment protection, and agreed that mutually beneficial cooperation should be undertaken in this field including the transfer of environmentally-sound technology to promote sustainable development. The Meeting agreed to strengthen cooperation between the two regions to deal with the illicit drug trade, money laundering, terrorism and other international crimes, including exploitation of illegal immigration, both bilaterally and through existing multilateral initiatives.

17. The Meeting called for the strengthening of cultural links between Asia and Europe, particularly the fostering of closer people-to-people contacts, which is indispensable to the promotion of greater awareness and understanding between the peoples of both regions. The Meeting emphasized that these new links between Asia and Europe should help overcome misperceptions that may exist between the two regions, and could be further reinforced through promoting cultural, artistic, educational activities and exchanges involving particularly youth and students, and tourism between the two sides. In this respect, the Meeting was informed about the results of the Europe-Asia Forum on culture, values and technology, recently held in Venice. The Meeting also encouraged cooperation in the preservation of cultural heritage.

Future Course of ASEM

18. The Meeting regarded the ASEM as a useful process for promoting further cooperation between Asia and Europe. The Meeting recognized that the ASEM process needed to be open and evolutionary. The Meeting agreed that intersessional activities are necessary although they need not be institutionalized. The Meeting further agreed that follow-up actions to be undertaken jointly by the participants to the ASEM would be based on consensus. The Meeting also agreed to facilitate cooperation between Asian and European business leaders.

19. The Meeting agreed to the following follow-up measures:

- The Foreign Ministers and the Senior Officials' Meeting in charge of the First ASEM would coordinate and prepare for the Second ASEM on the basis of the result of the First ASEM. In this connection, a Foreign Ministers' Meeting would be held in 1997;
- An Economic Ministers' Meeting would be held in Japan in 1997 to discuss relevant
- economic issues;
- An informal Senior Officials' meeting would be held in Brussels in July 1996 on ways to promote economic cooperation between the two regions, and in particular liberalization and facilitation of trade and investments, with an initial emphasis on WTO issues;
- A Meeting of Government and Private Sector Working Group would be convened in Thailand to draw up within six months an Asia-Europe Investment Promotion Action Plan to promote greater cross-flows of investment between Asia and Europe. Such a group could also study the current status of, and potentials for, investment between Asia and Europe and recommend measures to be taken in this regard;
- An Asia-Europe Business Forum would hold its inaugural meeting in France in 1996 and the next meeting in Thailand. At this Forum, Senior Officials would consider the appropriate modalities for fostering greater cooperation between the business and private sectors of the two regions. In this connection, a business conference would be held in 1997;
- Malaysia would act as coordinator for the study of integrating a Trans-Asian railway network (commencing initially with the railway project of the Mekong Basin Development) and also the study of the possible subsequent integration of this railway network with the Trans-European railway network;

- The establishment in Thailand of an Asia-Europe Environmental Technology Centre to under take research and development activities as well as provide policy guidance to both regions' governments and peoples;
- An Asia-Europe Foundation would be set up in Singapore with contributions from Asian and European countries, to promote exchanges between think-tanks, peoples and cultural groups. In this connection, Singapore has offered to contribute US$ 1 million to seed this foundation;
- An Asia-Europe University Programme would be started to foster exchanges of students and scholars with a view to developing better understanding of the cultures, histories and business practices of both regions;
- Intellectual exchanges between Asia and Europe through the holding of seminars and symposia on international and regional issues and the establishment of networks among the appropriate think-tanks from both regions;
- Objective studies on the economic synergy between Asia and Europe to provide future prospects and a solid basis for development-effective policy measures;
- Youth exchange programmes of mini "Davis-type" to strengthen cultural links and the mutual understanding between the two regions.

The Meeting also agreed to consider the following:

- A Meeting of Finance Ministers;
- An Asia-Europe Cooperation Framework which will spell out the principles and mechanisms for long-term Asia-Europe cooperation in political, economic, social and other areas;
- The establishment of a study group on enhancing technological exchanges and cooperation, particularly in the areas of agriculture, environmental protection, and technological upgrading and improvement of enterprises;
- The development of closer cooperation among customs authorities in Asia and Europe in the areas of customs procedure and prevention of illicit drug trade;
- Cooperation in the development of the Mekong River Basin.

20. The Meeting agreed to hold the Second ASEM in two years' time in the United Kingdom and the Third ASEM in the Republic of Korea in the year 2000.

Information Copyright © 1996 Ministry of Foreign Affairs, Thailand.

ANNEX 2

ASEM 2: CHAIRMAN'S STATEMENT 1998

INTRODUCTION

1. The Second Asia-Europe Meeting (ASEM 2) was held in London on 3-4- April 1998. It was attended by Heads of State and Government from ten Asian and fifteen European nations and the President of the European Commission under the Chairmanship of the Prime Minster of the United Kingdom of Great Britain and Northern Ireland acting also as President of the Council of the European Union. Leaders were accompanied by their Foreign Ministers, members of the European Commission and other Ministers.

2. Leaders recalled their first Summit in Bangkok on 1-2 March 1996 (ASEM 1) when they resolved to build on the success of that Meeting by convening again in London in 1998 and in Seoul in 2000. They reviewed with satisfaction the progress made since their first Meeting in strengthening links between Asia and Europe. They reaffirmed, in a highly interdependent world, the role of ASEM in reinforcing the partnership between Europe and Asia in the political, economic, cultural and other areas of cooperation.

3. Drawing on the conclusions of the inaugural Bangkok Summit and consistent with the agreed Asia-Europe Cooperation Framework Paper. Leaders confirmed that the ASEM process should:

be conducted on a basis of equal partnership, mutual respect and mutual benefit;
be an open and evolutionary process: enlargement should be conducted on the basis of consensus by the Heads of State and Government;
enhance mutual understanding and awareness through a process of dialogue and lead to cooperation on the identification of priorities for concerted and supportive action;
carry forward the three key dimensions with the same impetus: fostering political dialogue, reinforcing economic cooperation and promoting cooperation in other areas;
as an informal process. ASEM need not be institutionalized. It should stimulate and facilitate progress in other forms: go beyond governments in order to promote dialogue and cooperation between the business/private sectors of the two regions and, no less importantly, between the peoples of the two regions;

ASEM should also encourage the cooperative activities of think tanks and research groups of both regions.

With this in mind Leaders also welcomed the discussions at the Meetings of Foreign, Economic and Financial Ministers.

DEVELOPMENT IN THE TWO REGIONS

4. Leaders attached high importance to remedying the financial and economic situation in Asia and reaffirmed their commitment to working together to address this global concern. To this end, a separate statement has been issued to the financial and economic situation in Asia which contains ideas and concrete initiatives on this matter.

5. Leaders discussed the progress made towards achieving European Economic and Monetary Union (EMU) as well as the launching of a European Union enlargement process. They noted the EU's firm intention that this would not lead to an inward-looking approach. They expected that the successful introduction of the euro would contribute to growth and stability of both Europe and the rest of the world.

6. Leaders recognized the growing interdependence of the economics and economic policies of the ASEM countries and agreed on the importance of deepening dialogue and cooperation between Asia and Europe. In this context, they welcomed the strengthened dialogue among the Finance Ministers and their Deputies on macroeconomic and financial issues including the opportunities and challenges presented by the introduction of the euro. In addition they agreed to cooperate to help their business communities prepare fully for the introduction of the euro.

7. Leaders noted that ASEAN celebrated its 30th Anniversary in 1997 by moving closer towards achieving the goal of embracing all nations in Southeast Asia ("ASEAN 10") with the admission of two new members. They welcomed the positive role played by ASEAN, with the cooperation of all its Dialogue Partners, in enhancing regional peace and stability, growth, and social progress.

8. Leaders noted the outcome of the informal ASEAN Summit held in Kuala Lumpur in December 1997, including the adoption of the ASEAN Vision 2020. Leaders also noted the outcome of the informal meetings between leaders of ASEAN and the leaders of China, Japan and the Republic of Korea which have contributed to closer dialogue and cooperation within the region.

FOSTERING POLITICAL DIALOGUE

9. Leaders noted that the first meeting of ASEM Foreign Ministers in Singapore in February 1997 and subsequent meetings of Senior Officials had been the occasion for useful discussions of regional and international issues of common interest, and had contributed to the enhancement of understanding and friendship through a comprehensive political dialogue guided by the principles laid down by Leaders in Bangkok in 1996 and reflected in the paragraphs 5, 6, and 7 of the Bangkok Chairman's Statement.

Leaders noted with approval the expansion of Asia-Europe dialogues on general security issues. The ASEAN Regional Forum has carved an important role for itself in the discussion of regional security issues, and Leaders welcomed the substantial work already accomplished on confidence-building measures. They looked forward to the ASEAN Post Ministerial Conference in Manila in July.

Leaders confirmed their resolve to pursue global political issues. They welcomed progress achieved already in work to promote effective UN institutional reform, with particular reference to the Secretary-General's Track II reform package and reaffirmed their continued commitment to cooperate in promoting reform with a view to reinforcing its pre-eminent role in maintaining and promoting international peace and security and sustainable development. Leaders took note of recent positive developments in the spheres of arms control, disarmament and non-proliferation, including the entry into force of the Chemical Weapons Convention and the opening for signature of the Comprehensive Test Ban Treaty. They underlined the importance of strengthening global initiatives and their determination to deepen ASEM cooperation in these fields. Leaders reaffirmed their support for: the negotiations on measures to strengthen the Biological and Toxin Weapons Convention; an early start to negotiations in the Conference on Disarmament on fissile material cut-off on the basis of the agreed mandate; and the early entry into force of and progress towards the goals stated in the Comprehensive Test Ban Treaty.

Leaders confirmed their commitment to pursue and stable international environment. In an increasingly interdependent world where regional problems could have world-wide impact members of the international community are required to tackle those problems jointly. From this standpoint, Leaders discussed regional and international issues of common interest such as the situations in Cambodia, the Korean peninsula, in Bosnia and Kosovo, and enlargement of the EU. They expressed their opposition to all forms of racism and xenophobia, and agreed to intensify their efforts to contribute to peace, stability and prosperity through cooperation between Asia and Europe.

REINFORCING ECONOMIC COOPERATION

10. Leaders noted with satisfaction the substantial progress made since Bangkok in the furtherance of ASEM cooperation in the economic field, which forms the basis for a strong partnership between Asia and Europe. They welcomed various initiatives agreed at the first Economic Minister's Meeting in Makuhari. They looked forward to the early implementation of the Investment Promotion Action Plan (IPAP), and of the Trade Facilitation Action Plan (TFAP), now adopted, and tasked Economic Ministers to supervise the implementation closely, recognizing the economic diversity within and between Asia and Europe. Leaders also recognized the important role of investment in promoting growth in the two regions, and recalled the importance of programmes designed to promote two-way trade and investment between ASEM partners. They encouraged business to play an active part in the restoration of economic confidence and growth in the affected Asian countries, and to maintain and extend business investment activities in both regions. They welcomed all measures and initiatives designed to stimulate and facilitate two-way trade and investment flows.

11. Leaders emphasized the important contribution that increased trade and investment, based on open markets and firm adherence to applicable international rules could make to the early restoration of broad-based economic growth in the Asian region, as evidenced by the important achievements in the growth of the world economy which the development of the multilateral trading system had made possible over the past fifty years. They agreed to strengthen further the World Trade Organization as the main forum for negotiation and to provide the means for further global liberalization of trade within the multilateral framework. In this regard, they reaffirmed the importance of fully implementing all existing WTO commitments, including through fulfilment of the built-in agenda according to agreed timetables, and underlined their willingness to cooperate in making the WTO Ministerial Conference in Geneva this year a success, and to prepare an agenda for the next Ministerial Conference with a view to pursuing further trade liberalization.

12. Leaders agreed that it was essential in a highly integrated world economy that all trading nations were members of the WTO. They stressed that full participation in the WTO by ASEM partners will strengthen the organization, and undertook to steps up efforts in that direction with a view to obtaining an early accession of these

nations to the WTO on the basis of congruous market access commitments and adherence to the WTO rules.

13. Leaders reaffirmed the important role of the business/private sector in strengthening economic linkages between Asia and Europe, and acknowledged the particular contribution made to this process by the Asia-Europe Business Forum since its inaugural meeting in Paris in October 1996. Noting with satisfaction the evidence of deepening business/private sector engagement in the ASEM process provided by the second Business Forum in Bangkok, the Leaders welcomed the opportunity afforded by the third Business Forum in London both to build on the success of the Paris and Bangkok meetings and for the first time to bring ASEM Leaders and senior business representatives into direct dialogue. They expressed the need for the ABEF to continue the momentum of business-to-business exchanges created by the Asia-Europe Business Conference in Jakarta in 1997. Acknowledging the special needs of small and medium sized enterprises, Leaders looked forward to the Asia-Europe SME Conference to be held in Naples in May 1998 and further initiatives designed to foster full participation of SMEs in the ASEM process.

14. Since science and technology has increasingly become the key factor and chief engine for economic growth, and there is enormous potential for mutually-beneficial cooperation between Asia and Europe. Leaders noted various follow-up activities in this field and called for further efforts to strengthen technological cooperation between Asia and Europe. In this connection, a possible meeting of ministers for Science and Technology was discussed by Leaders.

14bis. Leaders further agreed that they should do more, collectively, to enlarge understanding of the consequences of the present crisis, including sending high-level business missions to the region for the purpose of encouraging investment. They underlined the importance of generating global confidence in the future of Asia's economies.

PROMOTING COOPERATION ON GLOBAL ISSUES

15. Leaders reintegrated the importance which they attached to enhancing the ASEM dialogue on global issues such as human resource development, including management education, the fight against poverty, food supply, improvement of community health, employment, protection of the environment and promotion of the welfare of women and children. They welcomed a series of new initiatives proposed in these areas. In this respect, Leaders supported International Development

Cooperations Targets including those agreed in various UN conferences, in particular the target to reduce by one half the proportion of people living in extreme poverty by the year 2015, as the basis for a collaborative international effort to eliminate poverty and to improve the living conditions of poor people.

16. Recalling the critical challenge posed by climate change. Leaders welcomed the Kyoto Protocol as an important step forward. They underlined the need for rapid follow-up in preparation for the Buenos Aires Conference in November 1998.

17. Leaders agreed that addressing the issue of money laundering will continue to transparency of the financial systems and to efforts to combat drug trafficking and organized crime by attacking criminal assets. The development of policies against money laundering has been helped by the PAFT's 40 Recommendations which are now an internationally accepted standard. They looked forward on enhanced cooperation between Europe and Asia in this area, including exchanges of experts and a joint study on organized crime's links with Asian and Western financial markets. They asked Finance Ministers to encourage this cooperation and review progress at their next meeting.

18. Leaders highlighted the importance of international cooperation to ensure that computer systems are millennium compliant particularly in sectors where system failures arising from the Y2K problem could cause social and economic dislocation.

PROMOTING COOPERATION IN SOCIAL AND CULTURAL ISSUES

19. Leaders affirmed the importance they attached to developing initiatives in the cultural and social fields in order to diversify further Asia-Europe Cooperation. They agreed that these initiatives should respond to and encourage the wide interest in strengthening links between the two regions shown by the public, think-tanks, research groups, universities and all sectors of society generally, thereby promoting the human dimension in ASEM.

20. Leaders welcomed the establishment of the Asia-Europe Foundation and commended its work in promoting people-to-people contacts and enhanced intellectual and cultural exchange between the two regions. They welcomed the Foundation's initiatives such as the first Asia-Europe Young Leaders' Symposium, co-sponsored with Japan: the Editors' Roundtable in Luxembourg; the Cultural Forum in Paris; the Asia-Europe Lecture series; the first Europe-Asia Forum in Singapore; the launching of an ASEF website, the programme of cultural and arts

events which will be held around ASEM 2. Leaders reaffirmed their support for the Foundation and recommended to their national institutions, corporations and other relevant non-governmental organizations that they cooperate with the Foundation.

TAKING FORWARD THE ASEM PROCESS

21. Building on the conclusions of ASEM 1 held in Bangkok, Leaders:
   decided that discussions should continue on the timing and modalities concerning the expansion of membership,
   commissioned an Asia-Europe Vision Group to develop a medium- to long-term vision to help guide the ASEM process into the 21st century. Leaders noted that the Vision Group will hold the first meeting in Cambridge on 6 April 1998, and will submit its report to Foreign Ministers in 1999 then to ASEM 3 along with the Ministers' views on its recommendations,
   adopted a Asia-Europe Cooperation Framework (AECF) to guide, focus and coordinate ASEM activities in political dialogue, the economic and financial fields and other areas,
   adopted a Trade Facilitation Action Plan (TFAP) and an Investment Promotion Actions Plan (IPAP), including the establishment of an Investment Experts Group (IEG),
   launched an Asia-Europe Environmental Technology Centre to located in Thailand,
   emphasized the importance of continued work to develop policies and measures for cooperation on the other relevant fields such as infrastructure development, energy and the environmental sector with the objective of promoting sustainable economic growth,
   welcomed the holding of further Asia-Europe Young Leaders Symposia in Baden/Vienna, Austria on 24-29 May 1998 and in the Republic of Korea in 1999 and Business Fora in Korea in 1999, in Austria in 2000 and in Singapore in 2001,
   welcomed the establishment of the Asia-Europe Centre at the University of Malaya, Kuala Lumpur, Malaysia and took note of the intention to upgrade it to an Asia-Europe University,
   took note of a report on the Trans-Asian railway project coordinated by Malaysia.

22. Taking forward cooperation on major themes identified at ASEM 1 in Bangkok and in line with the priorities outlined in the Asia-Europe Cooperation Framework, Leaders endorsed new initiatives to:

ANNEX 2: CHAIRMAN'S STATEMENT 1998

- hold an Asia-Europe Small and Medium-sized Conference in Naples on 28-30 May 1998;
- established the ASEM Connect electronic resource network for SMEs;
- promote the welfare of children. A meeting of experts in the UK in October 1998 will develop practical cooperation on child welfare issues, including the fight against commercial sexual exploitation of children;
- cooperate in combated illicit drugs, in particular to prevent the diversion of precursor chemicals and to support and encourage action against synthetic drugs;
- enhance and expand educational links in order to enable young people of the two regions to work together on common problems and projects as demonstrated by the pilot project involving young people in vocational training in schools in ASEM countries;
- strengthen cooperation on environmental issues with particular emphasis on: fresh water, forestry, climate change and sustainable development - including follow-up and implementation of the Rio Agreements, of Agenda 21, the Framework conventions on biodiversity and climate change, including follow-up to the outcome of the Kyoto Conference, and the Statement of Principles on Forests;
- take forward work in cooperation on environmental disaster preparedness including both short and long-term programmes, such as DIPECHO, to strengthen environmental disaster management capacities in Southeast Asia to enable countries to cope better with the threats posed by disasters affecting the natural environment including forest.

Leaders took note of the following new activities and encouraged their further development within the context of the Asia-Europe Cooperation Framework:
- Protecting and promoting cultural heritage in ASEM countries, building on the conference/seminar to be held in London in May 1998. And ad hoc working group will meet in Vietnam in the autumn of 1998 to draft a relevant plan of action for the effective implementation of this initiative from 1999 onwards;
- holding of a seminar on the roles of the State and the market in Copenhagen before the Foreign Ministers' Meeting in 1999;
- promoting cooperation in information technology and telecommunications between Asia and Europe for better understanding and mutual benefits through setting up of an Asia-Europe Information Technology and Telecommunications Programme (AEITTP) to be coordinated by Thailand;
- cooperation in improving community health care. A seminar of experts in Vietnam, in the third quarter of 1998 will discuss Asia-Europe cooperation in combining traditional and modern medicine and treatment for community health care;

- establishing a network of megacities of ASEM Partners to exchange views, information and experiences as well as to extend technical cooperation to support the sustainable development of these megacities. To this end, the first Asia Europe Forum of Governors of Cities (AEFGC) will be held in Thailand in 1999. This initiative as well as Singapore's initiative in convening a World Conference on Model Cities in 1999 would contribute to the success of the World Conference on Sustainable Urban Development which would be held in Berlin in the Year 2000;
- The establishment of ASEM Education hubs to encourage more academic exchanges between student of Asian and European Universities;
- promoting exchanging of views and cooperation on the issue of sustainable agriculture through the setting up of an Asia-Europe Agricultural Forum (AEAF);
- the proposal from the Bangkok Business forum for the establishment where appropriate of SME centres;
- establishing an Asia-Europe Management programme at the Asian Institute of Management;
- a Seminar on Labour Relations to be held in the Hague in October 1998, back-to-back with the ASEF Board of Governors' meeting at the time;
- the holding of a Seminar in the Philippines on 'peace and society building' in areas that have been going through crisis and turmoil and whose development is the linchpin of efforts to maintain peace.

TOWARDS ASEM 3 AND BEYOND

23. Leaders confirmed their intention to meet again at ASEM 3 in Seoul, the Republic of Korea, in 2000, and decided to hold the Fourth ASEM meeting in Europe in 2002. They noted that Foreign Economic and Finance Ministers would meet in Germany in 1999 before ASEM 3.

London, 4 April 1998

ANNEX 3

ASEM 2: STATEMENT ON THE FINANCIAL AND ECONOMIC SITUATION IN ASIA

A SHARED INTEREST IN RESTORING STABILITY

1. Leaders discussed the recent financial and economic situation in Asia, emphasizing its impact on the global economy and stressing their concern about the human cost to the people of Asia. They reaffirmed the need to respond decisively to the crisis and welcomed the reforms being undertaken by the Asian countries concerned to promote financial and economic stability. They expressed confidence that with full implementation of the necessary policy reforms and strong mutual support financial stability would be restored. Strong economic fundamentals would enable Asia's impressive growth performance to continue over the medium term. Leaders noted Europe's deep interest in the resolution of Asia's financial difficulties and full participation in multilateral and bilateral efforts to overcome the current problems. They also took note of the significant financial and economic support provided by Asian Partners.

REFORM IN ASIA MATCHED BY SUPPORT FROM THE INTERNATIONAL COMMUNITY

2. Leaders agreed that it was important to reinforce the role of the International Monetary Fund at the centre of the global response to what is the global concern. They expressed their strong support for full implementation of the programmes of reform agreed with the IMF, the World Bank and the Asian Development Bank, which would be vital in restoring confidence in Asian economies and financial markets. They appreciated and encouraged the adjustment efforts in the Asian countries concerned. They emphasized that policies should be implemented in an open, transparent and non-discriminatory manner.

3. Leaders welcomed the timely response to date to the crisis from the international community. They recognized the considerable financial assistance provided through the International Financial Institutions as well as various supplementary bilateral arrangements to help the Asian countries concerned. In particular, they supported the provision of high levels of IMF resources in support of strong programmes of adjustment, and welcomed the creation of the new IMF Supplement Reserve Facility.

REFORMING AND STRENGTHENING THE INTERNATIONAL FINANCIAL SYSTEM FOR STABILITY

4. Leaders discussed ways, including those contained in the Manila Framework, in which the international monetary and financial system could be reformed and strengthened, focusing on crisis prevention and reducing the vulnerability of domestic financial systems to potential shocks, including speculation-induced instability. They called for:

a strengthened capacity of the IMF to respond to financial difficulties in a timely and decisive manner, and access to expanded levels of IMF resources through a quota increase and early ratification of the New Arrangements to Borrow (NAB).

enhanced and more transparent global IMF surveillance, complemented in Asia by the establishment of a new regional surveillance mechanism.

strengthened cooperation, regulation and supervision in financial sectors, and an examination by the IMF and international regulators' bodies of ways to improve transparency in financial and capital markets, including the possibility of monitoring short-term capital flows.

PRIVATE SECTOR INVOLVEMENT

5. Leaders stressed the importance of devising strategies to secure private sector involvement in providing financial assistance as necessary and appropriate, in cooperation with and supporting the approach of the public sector. They noted in particular the importance of private sector involvement in the successful conclusion of debtor/creditor fora and provision of trade credit in various countries. They appreciated the constructive role played by European, Asian and other commercial banks in this regard. They also agreed on the importance of providing the right climate for private investors to make full and adequate assessments in relation to their lending and financing decisions. Leaders also recognized that the increased contact and exchange of information between the public and private sector could contribute to preventing potential financial difficulties.

EXPORT FINANCE

6. Leaders recognized the importance of continued access to trade finance for economic recovery within the framework set by the IMF. They welcomed the proposals made by major export credit agencies (ECAs) during the course of the G7 Finance Ministers and Central Bank Governors meeting, 20 February 1998, and subsequently by other countries, to provide trade financing facilities in Asia. They encouraged further ECAs to provide special credit facilities in order to

ease the shortage of liquidity of the export sectors of the Asian countries concerned.

TECHNICAL COOPERATION

7. Leaders agreed that co-operation through ASEM on technical assistance could play a major role in support of the programmes of reform agreed with the international financial institutions. They welcomed the creation of an ASEM trust fund at the World Bank to help finance technical assistance and advice both on restructuring the financial sector and on finding effective ways to redress poverty, drawing on European and Asian expertise. They also welcomed the recent enhancement of financial allocations by an Asian ASEM partner in the existing trust funds at the World Bank and Asian Development Bank for technical assistance in these areas.

8. In addition to existing bilateral arrangements, Leaders welcomed the proposal to create a European network, associating Asian expertise, for increasing the quality and quantity of technical advice in reforming the financial sector. They encouraged their financial supervisors to increase cooperation.

STRENGTHENING NATIONAL ECONOMIC SYSTEMS

9. Leaders noted the particular importance of strengthening and reforming financial systems and economic structures including corporate sectors, in order to realize Asia's underlying potential and achieve sustained economic development. They also noted that Asian efforts to undertake the necessary reforms in the financial sector could play a decisive role in restoring investors' confidence by ensuring transparency, predictability, and proper surveillance. Cooperation among ASEM partners in human resources development, promotion of SMEs, technical assistance and improvement of the investment environment should play a major role in strengthening the economic base. Leaders asked the relevant authorities to liaise closely with the Asia-Europe Business Forum (AEBF) in considering and, where appropriate, developing proposals for promoting SMEs.

REDUCING THE SOCIAL IMPACT

10. Leaders recognized the need to consider the social impact of the financial difficulties in Asia. They noted that implementing comprehensive reform programmes offered the opportunity to build a strong platform for sustainable future growth. But in doing so, it would be important to protect social

expenditure wherever possible, and develop well-designed and affordable social safety nets to safeguard the poor.

11. Aware of the importance of complementarity between economic and social policies, they agreed to adopt a balanced approach in addressing the socio-economic impact. They supported the efforts of the World Bank and Asian Development Bank in this respect, and welcomed the poverty focus of the new and existing trust funds at these institutions.

IMPACT ON THE WORLD ECONOMY

12. Leaders also considered the impact of Asia's current difficulties on the world economy. They noted that with continued implementation of sound economic and financial policies, the overall impact on the world economy was likely to be material but manageable. There were already signs of substantial improvements in the external accounts of some Asian countries, but the difficulties were not yet over and the need for vigilance remained.

13. While expressing confidence about the proposals for recovery in Asia, all ASEM partners recognized the need to take appropriate measures to strengthen consumer and business confidence in order to overcome the crisis. It was also important more than ever for global economic stability for the European countries to keep their own economies in good order.

IMPORTANCE OF MAINTAINING AN OPEN TRADING SYSTEM

14. Leaders acknowledged that the crisis could trigger protectionist reaction as a result of shifts in trade and investment flows or of requirements for adjustment. They expressed their common resolve to resist any protectionist pressure and at least to maintain the current level of market access while pursuing further multilateral liberalization, which was recognized as the most effective means of overcoming protectionist pressures and helping to alleviate the crisis. They undertook not to take any restrictive measures in the legitimate exercise of their WTO rights that would go beyond that which is necessary to remedy specific situations, as provided for in WTO rules. Acknowledging that the trade and investment pledge applied to all ASEM partners, Leaders also invited trading partners outside ASEM to join in this pledge.

15. Leaders also acknowledged the vital contribution of economic reform programmes, including reforms in the financial sector in Asia, to global efforts to resist protectionism, stimulate investment and strengthen the international trading system.

16. They noted that development in Asian markets could lead to a drop in investments in both directions and pledge to do their best to facilitate the maintenance and expansion of FDI. They urged full and rapid implementation by all ASEM partners of the Trade Facilitation Action Plan and the Investment Promotion Action Plan in order further to open up trade and expand investment between Asia and Europe.

FUTURE COOPERATION

17. Leaders agreed that these issues should be followed up vigorously and asked their Finance Ministers and their Economic Ministers to consider concrete measures to deal with them.

London, 3 April 1998.

ANNEX 4

CONTRIBUTORS

DEREK FATCHETT is the Minister of State for Foreign and Commonwealth Affairs and member of Parliament for Leeds Central.

ANDRÁS HERNÁDI is Director of the Japan East and Southeast Asia Research Centre at the Institute for World Economics of the Hungarian Academy of Sciences in Budapest.

MICHAEL HINDLEY is a Labour Member of the European Parliament for Lancashire South since 1984 and is a member of the External Economic Affairs Committee.

TETSUNDO IWAKUNI is a member of the House of Representatives in Tokyo.

JONG BUM KIM is a Research Fellow at the Korea Institute for International Economic Policy, a public policy think-tank in Seoul.

CÉSAR DE PRADO YEPES is Doctoral Researcher in the Department of Political and Social Sciences at the European University Institute, Florence.

JÜRGEN RÜLAND is Professor of International Policy and Development Cooperation at the University of Rostock.

GERALD SEGAL is a Senior Fellow at the International Institute for Strategic Studies and Director of the Economic and Social Research Council's Pacific Asia Programme.

DONG-IK SHIN is a member of the Diplomatic Service of the Republic of South Korea.

WIM STOKHOF is Director of the International Institute for Asian Studies, Leiden/Amsterdam, and Secretary of the European Science Foundation Asia Committee.

PAUL VAN DER VELDE is Head of Communications and Editor of the International Institute for Asian Studies, Leiden/Amsterdam, and Vice-Chairman of the Dutch Association for Asian and Pacific Studies.

CONTRIBUTERS

PERCY WESTERLUND is Director of Relations with Far Eastern Countries for the European Commission. He represents the Commission in the Group of Senior Officials, which prepares and coordinates ASEM activities.

ZHAO GANCHENG is a Research Fellow of the Shanghai Institute for International Studies.

ANNEX 5

ABBREVIATIONS

ADB	Asian Development Bank
AEAF	Asia-Europe Agricultural Forum
AEBF	Asia-Europe Business Forum
AECF	Asia-Europe Cooperation Framework
AEFGC	Asia-Europe Forum of Governors of Cities
AEITTP	Asia-Europe Information Technology and Telecommunications Programme
AFTA	ASEAN Free Trade Area
AMM	ASEAN Annual Ministerial Meeting
APEC	Asia-Pacific Economic Cooperation
ARF	ASEAN Regional Forum
ASEAN	Association of South East Asian Nations
ASEF	Asia-Europe Foundation
ASEM	Asia-Europe Meeting
BISTEC	Bangladesh, India, Sri Lanka and Thailand Economic Cooperation
CBMs	Confidence Building Measures
CEFTA	Central European Free Trade Agreement
DG	Directorate General
EAEC	East Asian Economic Caucus
EC	European Commission
ECAS	Export Credit Agencies
EFTA	European Free Trade Association
EIAS	European Institute for Asian Studies
EMM	Economic Ministers Meeting
EMU	European Economic and Monetary Union
EP	European Parliament
ESF	European Science Foundation
ETSI	European Telecommunications Standardization Institute
EU	European Union
EURATOM	European Atomic Organization
FDIs	Foreign Direct Investments
FPDA	Five Power Defence Arrangements
G-7	Grouping of top 7 industrialized countries
GATS	General Agreement on Trade in Services
GATT	General Agreement on Tariffs and Trade
GDP	Gross Domestic Product
GIP	Global Inventory Project
GIS	Global Information Society

ABBREVIATIONS

GNP	Gross National Product
IAEA	International Atomic Energy Agency
ICAS	International Convention of Asia Scholars
ICC	International Chamber of Commerce
IEC	International Electro-technical Commission
IEG	Investment Experts Group
IET	Interest Equalization Tax
IFOR	Peace Implementation Force
IIAS	International Institute for Asian Studies
IMF	International Monetary Fund
IPAP	Investment Promotion Action Plan
IOR	Indian Ocean Rim
IOR-ARC	Indian Ocean Rim Association for Regional Cooperation
ISDR	Institute for Security and Development Studies
ISO	International Organization for Standardization
ITU	International Telecommunications Union
KEDO	Korean Peninsula Economic Development Organization
MAI	Multilateral Agreement on Investment
MERCOSUR	Mercado Comun de Sul (Southern Common Market)
MFN	Most Favoured Nation
NAFTA	North American Free Trade Agreement
NATO	North Atlantic Treaty Organization
NICs	Newly Industrialized Countries
NIEs	Newly Industrializing Economies
NPT	Nuclear Non Proliferation Treaty
OAS	Organization of American States
OECD	Organization of Economic Cooperation and Development
OSCE	Organization of Security and Cooperation in Europe
PEARL	Programme for Europe-Asia Research Linkages
PMCs	Post-Ministerial Conferences
PRC	People's Republic of China
SAARC	South Asian Association for Regional Cooperation
SLORC	State Law and Order Restoration Council
SME	Small and Medium size Enterprise
SOMTI	Senior Officers Meeting on Trade and Investment
TAFTA	Transatlantic Free Trade Area
TFAP	Trade Facilitation Action Plan
UHDR	Universal Declaration of Human Rights
UN	United Nations
UNDP	United Nations Development Programme
UNESCO	United Nations Educational, Scientific and Cultural Organization
WIPO	World Intellectual Property Organization
WTO	World Trade Organization